CORN

roasted, creamed, simmered + more

olwen woodier

Storey Books • Massachusetts

The mission of Storey Publishing is to serve our customers
by publishing practical information that encourages
personal independence in harmony with the environment.

Edited by Dianne Cutillo and Karen Levy
Wendy Palitz, Creative Director
Art Direction by Meredith Maker
Front cover photographs by Index Stock/Charlie Borland (left), ©Renee Cornet
Photography/StockFood (right), ©Len Mastri Photography, Inc./StockFood (center left),
©Paul Poplis/Envision (center right)
Back cover photographs by Index Stock/David Burch (center right), © Mark Ferri/Envision (left),
©Paul Poplis/Envision (right and spine), Index Stock/Barry Winiker (center left)
Cover & text design by Carole Goodman, Blue Anchor Design
Text production by Karin Stack, Susan Bernier, and Kelley Nesbit
Indexed by Nan Badgett
Copyright © 2002, 1987 by Olwen Woodier

The information in this book is accurate and complete to the best of our knowledge. All recommendations are made without guarantee on the part of the author or Storey Publishing. The author and the publisher disclaim any liability in connection with the use of this information. For additional information, please contact Storey Books, 210 MASS MoCA Way, North Adams, MA 01247.

Storey books are available for special premium and promotional uses and for customized editions. For further information, please call Storey's Custom Publishing Department at (800) 793-9396.

Corn was first published as *Corn Meals & More* in 1987. All of the information in the previous edition was reviewed and updated, and 68 new recipes were added.

Printed in the United States by Von Hoffmann Graphics
10 9 8 7 6 5 4 3 2 1

Library of Congress Cataloging-in-Publication Data

Woodier, Olwen, date.
   Corn : roasted, creamed, simmered, and more / Olwen Woodier. — rev. ed.
     p. cm.
   Includes index.
   ISBN 1-58017-454-X (acid-free paper)
     1. Cookery (Corn) I. Title.
TX809.M2 W663 2002
641.6'315—dc21
                                                  2002001141

contents

dedication and acknowledgments

To Wendy and Richard, my two main corn lovers.

A big thanks to all the people at Storey Books who made *Corn* a possibility. I feel fortunate to have collaborated with such a good crew. It takes a lot of work by a lot of people to get a book through the production line, into the stores, and into the public eye, and I couldn't have done it without your help.

Special thanks go to my editor Dianne Cutillo, whose creative editorial and organizational skills were the driving force behind this revision. She is an inspirational editor to work with. Project editor Karen Levy, for her Sherlock Holmesian instincts to sift through so many facts and details. Publicity manager Stephanie Taylor, and all the sales associates.

The following people, who generously shared their recipes: Brian and Margaret Ann Ball of The Red Fox Restaurant in Snowshoe, West Virginia; Susan Curtis, owner and director of the Santa Fe School of Cooking in Santa Fe, New Mexico; Ross Edwards; Michael Kramer, partner and executive chef of McCrady's restaurant in Charleston, South Carolina; Megan Moore of Moore Fine Food in Great Barrington, Massachusetts; Christy Velie, head chef at Café Atlántico in Washington, DC; and the Zurschmeide family of Great Country Farms in Bluemont, Virginia.

The following people and organizations, for furthering my education about corn: Tony Bratch, commercial horticulture specialist at Virginia Tech in Blackburn, Virginia; Debbie Dillion, urban horticulturist at Loudoun County Extension in Leesburg, Virginia; Cary Nalls of Nalls' Farm Market in Alexandria, Virginia; The National Corn Growers Association; state corn growers associations and associated state universities; Lori Warner at The Popcorn Institute in Chicago, Illinois; The Virginia Corn Growers Association; The Virginia Department of Agriculture and Consumer Services; and Bruce Zurschmeide.

preface

O beautiful for spacious skies,
For amber waves of grain,
For purple mountain majesties
Above the fruited plain!
America! America!
God shed His grace on thee
And crown thy good with brotherhood
From sea to shining sea!

When Katharine Lee Bates wrote these famous lines in 1893, she was on top of Pike's Peak in Colorado Springs. Looking down over the plains, she was overcome by the beauty of her country. Although the amber waves of grain she saw were most likely prairie grasses or acres of wheat, her evocation could easily apply to vast fields of corn with their golden tassels gleaming in the summer sun or bronzed corn stalks heavy with ears of dried ornamental corn.

With its bright green husk and ornamental golden tassel, corn has been a motif in American art since prehistoric times. In fact, there is no vegetable, or fruit, more exclusively American than corn. It is the symbol of our bountiful land and of summer's abundant harvest. Indeed, for thousands of years, the appearance of the first crop of ripe corn has been cause for celebration. Today, corn is celebrated throughout the world as a major food source for humans and animals. And with its myriad by-products, corn is the fiber in the fabric of life that binds the Americas to the rest of the world — from sea to shining sea and from the mountains to the plains.

the history of corn

corn is the only important grain indigenous to the Western Hemisphere, and its proliferation has sown the seeds of civilization throughout the Americas for thousands of years. The great civilizations of the Incas, Mayas, and Aztecs were founded on the cultivation of corn. Indeed, agriculture was at the very center of their religion. Corn was their life source, and they depended on the rain to make it grow. In the name of corn, the Aztec people sacrificed young women to two of their most important deities, the rain god, Tlaloc, and the corn goddess, Chicomecoatl.

Corn was also the staple grain of the North American Indians. They considered it a gift from their gods and referred to it as "Sacred Mother." Many rituals were developed to summon the rain to ensure a good harvest. (Although corn is somewhat drought resistant during its last stages of growth, rain is essential during the reproductive tasseling stage — when the silks emerge and the kernels begin to swell.) Native Americans called corn *mahiz,* which means "our life."

It was once common belief that corn had been brought to the New World from Asia during prehistoric migrations. In 1950, anthropologists discovered fossilized wild corn pollen 200 feet below Mexico City. Radiocarbon dating determined that the pollen was 80,000 years old, predating the arrival of human beings in the Western Hemisphere and proving that corn was indigenous to the North American continent. Other expeditions during the 1950s unearthed tiny, half-inch ears of *cultivated* corn that were carbon-dated to as early as circa 5000 B.C.E.

It took centuries for corn to be carried north from Mexico by Native Americans migrating to what would later be the Four Corners region of New Mexico and Arizona. The appearance of corn in that region around 1200 B.C.E. contributed to a dramatic increase in population as corn farming was adopted in the Southwest. It took several centuries more for corn to reach Native Americans living in what would become the northeastern United States.

In the 15th century, the Spanish discovered that corn was grown by many Native American tribes throughout the Americas — from the tip of South America to as far north as present-day Canada. Returning from a post in Cuba in 1492, a scouting party informed its leader, Christopher Columbus, that his *maíz* could be baked, dried, and ground into flour. Within a few years, *maize* was introduced to Europe. From Spain, it spread to France, Italy, Germany, Austria, and Eastern Europe; the Portuguese took maize seeds with them on their travels to Africa, the East Indies, and Asia. By the late 16th century, corn was grown in many corners of the world.

The British colonists in Jamestown, Virginia, would have starved to death in 1607 if they hadn't planted corn under the guidance of Captain John Smith, who had procured seeds from the Powhatan tribe. Hoping to find gold when they arrived, Smith's colony finally found it in the corn they grew. The people of Jamestown were so successful with their corn harvests that by 1630 they were exporting corn to Massachusetts and the Caribbean. During the late 17th century, when legal currency was insufficient to meet public demand, the Corn Exchange Bank was established and corn kernels were used in lieu of money.

The Native Americans' method of preserving maize under mounds of sand also saved the Pilgrims during their first winter in Massachusetts in 1620. When the *Mayflower* arrived at Plymouth, the Pilgrims were nearly devoid of supplies. Walking inland, they found a buried stash of corn, which not only fed them during that winter but also left them with enough kernels to plant in the spring. Learning from Native Americans, the settlers used corn in a variety of ways and, experimenting with the indigenous methods for making cornmeal breads, developed their own recipes.

Indian Wheat, of which there is three sorts, yellow, red, and blew...is light of digestion, and the English make a kind of Loblolly of it to eat with Milk, which they call Sampe; they beat it in a Mortar, and sift the flower out of it; the remainder they call Homminey, which they put into a Pot of two or three Gallons with water and boyl it upon a gentle Fire till it be like a Hasty Pudden; they put of this into Milk, and eat it. Their bread also they make a Homminey so boyled, and mixe their Flower with it.

—JOHN JOSSELYN, *writing about cornmeal mush and cornbread, which he called "New England Standing Dishes," 1670*

corn today

As a mainstay of the American diet, corn is a large part of agricultural business in the United States. Corn, as we know it today, is an annual plant with a sturdy, noded stalk that supports long, narrow leaves and multiple ears of corn. The male staminate flowers form the tassel at the top of the plant, and the female pistillate flowers develop into ovules and eventually the kernels on the cob. Enclosed in a leafy husk, the cob is pollinated by styles and stigmas, which extend outside the husk to form the silks. The strands of moist silks capture falling pollen grains and then transport them down to the cob to fertilize the ovules. When fertilization takes place, the ovules develop into plump, moist kernels.

Three parts of the kernel influence the color. The endosperm (the "germ" that nourishes the embryo) is made up of white, yellow, or orange-yellow pigments. The second layer of aleurone and the outer hull (the pericarp) may be blue, yellow, red, brown, or even colorless. Because the aleurone and the pericarp are translucent, the color of the endosperm shows through. The color we see is actually a combination of three pigmented layers.

Most of the corn grown in the United States comes from the Corn Belt states of Illinois, Iowa, Indiana, Missouri, Kansas, Ohio, Nebraska, Minnesota, Michigan, Wisconsin, and North and South Dakota. Although it has not been identified with certainty, it is considered a complex hybrid of several related New World grasses, including teosinte *(Zea* or *Euchlaena mexicana)*. There are four major commercial types of corn grown in the United States: dent corn, sweet corn, flint (Indian) corn, and popcorn. Dent, or field, corn *(Zea mays indentata)* has large ears, and the kernels, which have a soft starchy center, develop a dent on the crown at maturity. The most important commercial type of corn grown in the United States, dent corn is grown for animal feed, ethylene alcohol, breakfast flakes, corn syrup, and cornstarch.

Sweet corn *(Zea mays rugosa)* is eaten fresh, frozen, or canned. It stores its carbohydrates as sugar, which changes to starch as the corn ages. Sweet corn is harvested while the plant is still immature and the kernels are soft. Picking the corn speeds the conversion of sugar to starch (as does removing the husk). However, many sweet and supersweet varieties remain so for days after harvesting.

Flint, or Indian, corn *(Zea mays indurata)* got its name from its hard, smooth, flintlike kernel. This hard outer layer, however, surrounds a soft, starch endosperm. Indian corn is usually sold as decoration and is a favorite in the fall at roadside stands. It comes in blue, red, black, purple, orange, and multicolored varieties. Don't be misled by the colors, though — Indian corn is edible when ground and makes a sweet, high-protein cornmeal for breads, muffins, and pancakes. If the kernels are thoroughly dried, they can also be popped.

Popcorn *(Zea mays everta)* is the corn the Native Americans shared with the Pilgrims at the first Thanksgiving. The ears are short, and the kernels have a hard outer shell that surrounds a soft core of starch containing a small drop of water. When the kernels are heated, the water begins to expand and build pressure against the hard hull. As the kernel explodes, the soft, starchy center bursts and turns the hull inside out. There are three main types of commercial popcorn kernels: white, small yellow, and large yellow. Some varieties of popcorn, such as Bloody Butcher, Strawberry, and Multicolored Finger, are almost too pretty to pop, and most people use them for Thanksgiving and fall decorations.

Two other types of corn deserve mention. Flour corn is one of the oldest types of corn used by the Aztecs and Incas, who ground the soft kernels into flour. This corn has soft starch throughout with almost no hard endosperm. Because the kernels shrink uniformly during drying with little or no denting, they are easy to grind. Today, flour corn is grown primarily in the Andean region of South America. Baby corn is immature corn that is hand-harvested within one to five days (depending on the variety) after silks emerge from the ear tip. At this stage, the tiny, fingerlike ears are tender and delicately flavored, the entire cobs are edible, and the cobs can be frozen with great success. Several varieties, including Golden Midget, Glacier, Baby, Miniature Hybrid, Baby Asian, Baby Blue (blue popcorn ears), and Bo Peep (pink popcorn ears), are available for home gardening through various seed catalogs.

In addition to the major commercial varieties, specialty corns have been developed. Through genetics, plant breeders have altered the sugar, starch, protein, and oil content of corn to meet the needs of the food industry, livestock farmers, and other commercial corn users. Some specialty hybrids include blue and white corn, which are used in the production of foodstuffs, such as breads and tortillas. Other hybrids, including Everlasting Heritage, also known as Sugary Enhanced, have greater sugar contents and remain sweeter for longer periods of time. Other types, such as high-oil, nutritionally dense, and high-amylose corns, are grown for livestock feed.

And he gave it for his opinion, that whoever could make two ears of corn or two blades of grassto grow upon a spot of ground where only one grew before, would deserve better of mankind, and do more essential service to his country than the whole race of politicians put together.
—JONATHAN SWIFT, *Gulliver's Travels, 1726*

cooking with corn

Heap high the farmer's wintry hoard!
Heap high the golden corn!
No richer gift has Autumn poured
From out her lavish horn!
—JOHN GREENLEAF WHITTIER (1807–1892),
"The Corn Song"

corn can be mixed into just about any vegetable dish. It goes well with just one or two vegetables, such as tomatoes and squash, peas and beans, or sweet peppers and onions. It adds color, texture, and flavor to a large combination of vegetables, including onions, zucchini, peppers, tomatoes, and eggplant.

Although many people consider it at its best simply dropped into boiling water and rolled in butter, corn has a distinctive flavor that combines well with a mixture of other vegetables and seasonings. Here is one of my favorite combinations: Sauté 1 cup of chopped red bell pepper in olive oil for 3 minutes. Add 2 cups of corn kernels (fresh or canned and drained) and cook 2 minutes longer, until the mixture is hot. I vary the flavor of this dish with ½ teaspoon of dried basil or thyme or ¼ cup of chopped fresh chives.

buying

Whether you like your corn white, yellow, or bicolor or prefer the old-fashioned sweet varieties to the newer, supersweet ones, and whether you buy fresh-picked local corn from the farmers' market or shop in the produce section of a supermarket, there's only one way to select a prime ear of corn. Ideally, it should be cool, indicating that it has been kept under refrigeration. Choose ears with husks that are tightly wrapped, bright green, and slightly moist. Loose, yellowing husks indicate old, dry corn. The tassel may be dry, but it should be light colored and springy, not brown and stringy. The stem should be fresh and moist, not yellowed and dry.

Last, but most important, the kernels at the top should be plump, medium-sized (not too big and wide, not too small and narrow, and definitely not shriveled), close together, and glistening with moisture. To look at the kernels, peel the husk just a little bit on one side, but remember that someone will follow you and do the same. (On the farm, corn novices were taught to prick a kernel with a fingernail. If the juice looked like milk, the corn was fresh, sweet, and ready to eat. If the juice was clear, the corn was not ready; if there was no juice, it was old.) If the corn is organic, you may encounter a corn worm embedded in the kernels. Simply cut off the area around the worm and discard it, then cook the corn as usual.

If you don't eat all the corn the day you buy it, keep the extra ears unhusked in the refrigerator. If it's a supersweet variety, wrap the unhusked ears in damp paper towels and enclose them in a plastic bag. Refrigeration is critical for maintaining corn's freshness; when corn is kept at room temperature, its glucose converts to starch in as little as 24 hours. Old-fashioned sweet corn loses half of its glucose when kept at 80°F for 24 hours, but the newer, sweeter corn hybrids contain twice as much sugar and convert it to starch at a much slower rate, losing only 20 percent of their glucose when kept at 80°F for 24 hours. Refrigerated, unhusked corn will stay fresh and crisp for two to three days.

preparing

To husk corn, pull back the leaves as though peeling a banana and rip them off where they are attached to the stem. If the stem is long, snap it off with a quick flick of the hand or a sharp knife. Remove the silks by running your hands gently around the husked cob. If they are difficult to remove (some silks determinedly cling to the kernels), gently rub them off with a damp cloth.

If you want to remove the whole kernels from the cob, use a small, sharp knife to cut down the center of each row between the kernels and, working from top to bottom, scrape the kernels into a bowl. Some kitchen gadget stores sell a corn cutter that converts to a creamer to cut, shred, and scrape off the kernels, leaving the tough skins on the cob.

Here's a delicious recipe for fresh corn kernels. Melt 1 tablespoon of unsalted butter, add 2 cups of fresh kernels, and sauté for about 3 minutes over low heat. Sprinkle with salt and pepper. For standard sweet corn, you can dry-roast the kernels until they are golden brown. That way, they develop a nutty flavor and you won't notice that the sugar has turned to starch. I toss dry-roasted kernels into quesadillas, omelettes, relishes, soups, and salads.

putting up

If you grow your own corn or are able to buy superfresh corn from a farmers' market, you may want to extend the summer season by putting up — freezing, canning, preserving — the harvest for winter use. Even though you can buy commercially canned and frozen corn (and some of these products are excellent, with frozen corn usually having the edge on canned corn), there is something wonderful about being able to extend your own source of fresh, local produce — especially when you find a variety that you consider the sweetest and most flavorful you've ever tasted. The following simple instructions will get you started.

freezing

When freezing or canning, use the freshest sweet corn you can get your hands on. You can freeze whole ears of corn or just the kernels. If you plan to put up quarts of kernels or creamed corn, invest in a corn cutter to remove kernels effortlessly.

For whole ears of corn, heat a large pot of water until bubbles begin to form around the edges, then scald (do not boil) the ears for 3 minutes. Chill them immediately in cold running water, drain them, and freeze them in plastic bags. I like to use resealable plastic bags so I can squeeze all the air out, and I lay them in a single row in the freezer. That way, the ears don't stick together and I can remove one at a time. To cook the frozen ears, bring a pot of water to a rolling boil, drop the ears in, and cook for 2 minutes, until heated through or cooked to your liking. Defrosted ears generally take 1 to 2 minutes to heat through.

For whole kernels, heat a large pot of water until bubbles begin to form around the edges, then scald (do not boil) the whole ears for 1 minute. Chill them in cold running water and drain. Remove the kernels with a small, sharp knife or a corn cutter. Store the kernels in airtight containers or plastic bags and put them into the freezer. To serve the kernels as a fresh side dish, cook for 1 to 2 minutes if defrosted or 3 to 5 minutes if frozen.

For an easy method of creaming corn, remove the kernels with a small, sharp knife or a corn cutter. Measure the kernels and place them in a bowl. For each cup of kernels, add 1 teaspoon of cornstarch and mix thoroughly. Pour ¼ cup of low-fat milk per cup of kernels into a pan and bring to a boil. Stir the boiling milk into the kernel and cornstarch mixture. Return the mixture to the pan and simmer for 5 minutes, stirring frequently, until the creamed corn thickens. (Also see recipe on page 111.) Spoon into airtight plastic containers, leaving ½ inch of headroom, and freeze. Cook frozen or thawed creamed corn over low heat (or in a microwave) until heated through.

drying

When growing or buying corn for meal, flour, or popcorn, leave the ears on the stalks until the husks turn brown and the kernels are hard and dry. Remove the ears, pull back the husks, and tie two or three ears together. Hang them from a string strung across a room or store them in a basket in a warm, dry place. The kernels should rub off easily when they are thoroughly dry. The old method of drying corn is to cut the kernels from the cobs and place them in a single layer on a baking sheet. Place the sheet in a 250°F oven to dry slowly for 2 days. Stir the kernels occasionally. Store the oven-dried kernels in a cloth bag and hang the bag in a warm place. When thoroughly dry, the kernels can be stored in a glass jar with a tight-fitting lid for future use. Keep popcorn kernels in the refrigerator.

To reconstitute dried corn, soak the kernels in water (2 cups of water to 1 cup of corn) overnight, then simmer for 1 hour. Add a little butter, pepper, and cream to taste. One cup of dried corn makes 6 cups of reconstituted corn.

grinding

If you plan to make your own cornmeal, grind the dried kernels as you need them. How much corn you plan to grind will determine the type of mill you need. There are several types of grinders available for the job. For small amounts, a hand grinder or a blender will do a good job; for large quantities, you'll be better off with a power grinder. Cornmeal that has the germ left in it goes rancid quickly, so store it in plastic containers in the refrigerator or freezer. For more information, read about the commercial cornmeal grinding process on pages 144–145. For manufacturers and resources, see pages 181–183.

fertile crops

As a staple food crop, corn played an important role in the lives of Native Americans. They believed that when women planted corn, they passed along their fertility to the crops. In Longfellow's "The Song of Hiawatha," we learn that the Great Lakes Indians endowed corn with the spiritual force of the great god Mondamin.

> **All around the happy village**
> **Stood the maize-fields, green and shining,**
> **Waved the green plumes of Mondamin,**
> **Waved his soft and sunny tresses,**
> **Filling all the land with plenty.**

To ensure that Mondamin did a first-rate job of growing, Hiawatha instructed his wife, Minnehaha, to walk naked around the cornfields. While she chanted incantations to protect the corn from blight and insects, Hiawatha snared crows to prevent them from stealing the seedlings. In the Northeast, Native American women took care of the crows and other creatures by planting four corn seeds in each mound of earth. It is said that when Squanto, the Native American who taught the Plymouth Pilgrims how to grow corn, planted the four customary seeds, he chanted, "One for the squirrel, one for the crow, one for the cutworm, one for to grow."

In the Southwest, young Zuni warriors were instructed by their elders to "love and cherish your corn as you love and cherish your women." In other tribes, women allowed their hair to touch the earth where they planted corn. And stories abound of beautiful goddesses, such as the one who invited a young warrior to drag her by her hair across the scorched cornfields so that the corn would grow out of her body.

1

BREAKFASTS
& BREADS

nutritionists agree that the best way to boost morning energy and concentration is to eliminate foods that are high in sugar and replace them with those high in protein, and I have emphasized high-protein recipes in this chapter. Some recipes can be made quickly on weekday mornings. Others, though simple enough to make, are more suitable for weekends. Many lend themselves to reheating — for example, corn muffins, cornbreads, corn puddings, quiches, and polenta — in a toaster oven, microwave oven, or skillet, providing fast, high-protein breakfasts in minutes.

romanian *mamaliga*

Like oatmeal porridge, this version of cornmeal porridge is served hot and can be topped with butter, yogurt, sour cream, honey, or maple syrup. You can also convert this recipe into a polenta type of dish by spreading the porridge in a flat-bottomed pan, allowing it to cool, then cutting it into slices and frying them in hot butter for 1–2 minutes a side, until golden.

3 cups water

1 cup coarse cornmeal

1. Bring the water to a boil in a saucepan and slowly add the cornmeal in a thin stream, stirring constantly.

2. When the mixture is smooth, cover the pan and simmer for 10 minutes.

Yield: 4 servings

buttermilk cornmeal waffles

This basic buttermilk cornmeal recipe is for waffles, but you can use it for pancakes, too. I like to eat waffles with basted eggs or topped with blueberries and sliced bananas. However, they also taste delicious when sprinkled with sliced and seeded jalapeño chiles (wear gloves when handling chiles) and grated cheese and popped under the broiler for 1 minute.

¾ cup cornmeal

¾ cup presifted all-purpose flour

2 tablespoons sugar (optional)

½ teaspoon baking powder

½ teaspoon baking soda

½ teaspoon ground ginger (optional)

½ teaspoon salt

1 cup buttermilk

1 egg

3 tablespoons vegetable oil or melted butter

1. In a large bowl, mix the cornmeal, flour, sugar (if desired), baking powder, baking soda, ginger (if desired), and salt.

2. In a small bowl, beat together the buttermilk, egg, and oil until light and frothy.

3. Pour the buttermilk mixture into the cornmeal mixture and combine thoroughly. Spoon onto a lightly oiled hot waffle iron and cook for about 3 minutes, or until golden.

Yield: Ten 4-inch waffles

basic pancakes

This is my regular recipe, and I use whatever cornmeal I have on hand, which may be white, yellow, or blue — preferably stone-ground. This also doubles as waffle batter. Sometimes I add 1 cup of creamed corn and eliminate the oil or butter. Occasionally, I like to serve stuffed pancakes as a main dish. I make them with ¼ cup of batter and use them in place of tortillas for Chicken Enchiladas (see recipe on pages 118–119) or patty shells for Curried Chicken and Corn (see recipe on page 116). You can also add 1 cup of diced ham and scallions to the recipe for Creamed Corn (see page 111) and use that as a filling.

1⅓ cups low-fat milk

¾ cup all-purpose flour

½ cup cornmeal

2 eggs

2 tablespoons melted butter

¼ teaspoon ground nutmeg (optional)

2 tablespoons vegetable oil

1. Place all ingredients except the last 2 tablespoons of oil in a blender and blend for 1 minute, or beat by hand for 2 minutes.

2. Heat 1 tablespoon of the remaining oil in a large skillet and add about 2 tablespoons of batter for each pancake.

3. Cook over medium heat for 1–2 minutes on each side, or until golden brown.

4. Add the remaining tablespoon of oil to the skillet for the last batch of pancakes. (If you are making waffles, heat the waffle iron and cook each waffle for about 2 minutes.)

Yield: 4 servings

sour cream corn pancakes

1 cup frozen or canned corn kernels, crushed, or fresh corn kernels, scraped from the cob

½ cup all-purpose flour

¼ cup sour cream

2 eggs

4 tablespoons olive or vegetable oil

1. Beat together the corn, flour, sour cream, eggs, and 2 tablespoons of the oil.

2. Heat the remaining oil in a large skillet and drop in the batter 2 tablespoons at a time.

3. Cook over medium heat for 1½–2 minutes a side, until golden brown. Serve hot.

Yield: 4 servings

vegetable pancakes

1 cup chopped cooked vegetables or grated raw vegetables (for example: carrots, peppers, zucchini) or chopped fruit (for example: apples, peaches, pears)

1 cup low-fat milk

½ cup cornmeal

½ cup all-purpose flour

1 egg, beaten

3 tablespoons olive or vegetable oil

1. In a mixing bowl, combine the vegetables, milk, cornmeal, flour, egg, and 1 tablespoon of the oil.

2. Heat 1 tablespoon of the remaining oil in a large skillet and drop in large spoonfuls of the batter.

3. Cook over medium heat for about 2 minutes on each side, until golden brown. Repeat with the remaining oil and batter. Serve hot.

Yield: 6 servings

johnnycakes

Enjoy johnnycakes with butter and maple syrup or molasses and ham, bacon, or sausage. In Rhode Island, they are also served with applesauce, creamed codfish, or chipped beef. There are two versions: Newport County and South County, both made from stone-ground Rhode Island Whitecap flint corn. Both claim to be the very best. Judge for yourself.

newport county johnnycakes

1¾ cups cold milk

1 cup stone-ground white cornmeal

½ teaspoon salt

2 tablespoons vegetable oil or melted shortening

1. Combine the milk, cornmeal, and salt. The batter will be soupy.

2. Heat the oil on a griddle and ladle large spoonfuls of the batter onto it. The cakes should be about 5 inches in diameter.

3. Cook over medium heat for 2 minutes a side, or until golden brown.

Yield: 4 servings

south county johnnycakes

1 cup stone-ground white cornmeal

1 cup boiling water

1 teaspoon sugar or molasses (optional)

½ teaspoon salt

2 tablespoons vegetable oil or shortening

1. Blend the cornmeal, water, sugar (if desired), and salt.

2. Heat the oil on a griddle and drop large spoonfuls of the batter onto it. The cakes should be about 3 inches in diameter.

3. Cook over medium heat for 6 minutes on one side and 4 minutes on the other.

Yield: 4 servings

The rose may bloom for England,
  The lily for France unfold;
Ireland may honor the shamrock,
  Scotland her thistle bold:
But the shield of the great Republic,
  The glory of the West,
Shall bear a stalk of the tasseled Corn,
  Of all our wealth the best.
　—EDNA DEAN PROCTOR (1838–1923),
　　　　　　Columbia's Emblem

pones and puppies

Depending on your place of birth, you may eat hush puppies, pones, dodgers, oysters, flat cakes, toads, fritters, pancakes, or johnnycakes. Some of these names were derived from the shape or consistency of the product. Dodgers, for example, were dense and heavy, and the saying goes that if one were hurled your way, you'd be wise to dodge it. Corn oysters were shaped like oysters. Hush puppies evolved from a corn-hash mixture; as Southerners recount, they were thrown onto the floor to hush the puppies. Johnnycakes are from New England; their flat shape made them ideal food for a journey, so they were called journey cakes, and then johnnycakes.

skillet corn pancakes

For this recipe, you can substitute a shallow baking dish for the ovenproof skillet. And don't hesitate to substitute veggie-soy crumbles for the turkey bacon. I do when making this for myself or for my daughter, Wendy.

6 slices low-fat turkey bacon or ¾ cup veggie-soy crumbles

cooking oil spray (optional)

2 tablespoons olive or vegetable oil

1 cup corn kernels (drained if canned, thawed if frozen)

1 cup low-fat milk

⅔ cup all-purpose flour

⅓ cup whole wheat flour

2 eggs, separated

½ teaspoon freshly ground black pepper

1. Preheat oven to 450°F and have on hand an ovenproof skillet or use a 9- by 2-inch-deep baking dish.

2. In a skillet, cook the bacon for 4 minutes, or until crisp. Remove from the skillet and drain on paper towels. Crumble them into small pieces. If using veggie-soy crumbles, sauté in a skillet sprayed with cooking oil (I use olive oil spray).

3. Pour off and dispose of the bacon fat and put the oil into the ovenproof skillet. Place in the preheated oven.

4. Blend or process the corn, milk, all-purpose flour, whole wheat flour, egg yolks, and pepper for 30–40 seconds.

5. Beat the egg whites until stiff and stir into the corn mixture. Add the bacon.

6. Pour into the hot ovenproof skillet and bake for 15 minutes. Reduce the heat to 400°F and bake 10 minutes longer. Best when served warm.

Yield: 4–6 servings

corn oysters

There's practically nothing to these airy little cakes. Eat them for breakfast with maple syrup or serve them as a vegetable side dish. If you want to make real corn oysters — oysters folded into a light cornmeal batter and fried until golden — see the recipe on pages 92–93.

2 eggs, separated

1½ cups corn kernels, crushed (if using fresh corn, scrape it from the cob)

1 tablespoon low-fat milk

¼ cup all-purpose flour

¼ teaspoon coarsely ground black pepper, or 1 tablespoon sugar

2–4 tablespoons olive or vegetable oil

1. Beat the egg yolks in a large bowl; stir in the corn and milk.

2. Add the flour and pepper and combine.

3. Beat the egg whites until stiff and fold them into the batter.

4. Heat 2 tablespoons of the oil in a large skillet over medium to high heat. When hot, drop in tablespoons of the batter (don't crowd the pan) and cook approximately 1½ minutes per side, until golden crisp and puffy.

5. Add 1 tablespoon of the remaining oil to the pan, if necessary, for each batch. Serve hot.

Yield: 4 servings

breakfast burritos with corn tortillas

This recipe is a crowd pleaser on a brunch table. Arrange bowls of the ingredients and let each person assemble his or her own burrito. I often use flour tortillas in place of the heavier corn variety and serve salsa and sour cream on the side. To make a neater burrito that doesn't fall apart, place a moderate amount of filling in the center, then fold in the sides before rolling it up. When I do the assembling, I top the scrambled-egg filling with a spoonful each of salsa and sour cream before folding the tortilla.

12 eggs

½ teaspoon salt

½ teaspoon freshly ground black pepper

2 tablespoons olive or vegetable oil or melted butter

1 cup fresh, canned (drained), or frozen corn kernels

1 can (4–6 ounces) chopped green chiles, drained

1 cup grated Monterey Jack cheese

six 8-inch corn or flour tortillas

2–3 cups Tomato Salsa (see recipe on facing page)

¾ cup sour cream (optional)

1. Preheat the oven to 350°F.

2. In a large bowl, whisk together the eggs, salt, and pepper.

3. Heat the oil in a large skillet, add the corn and chiles, and cook over medium heat for 2–3 minutes.

4. Add the egg mixture and cook, stirring gently, until the eggs form soft curds, about 6–8 minutes.

5. Remove from the heat and stir in the cheese.

6. Warm the tortillas (see box on page 119).

7. To assemble each burrito, spoon about ⅓ cup of the egg mixture onto a tortilla and top with 2 tablespoons of salsa and 1 tablespoon of sour cream, if desired. Fold to enclose and eat out of hand.

Yield: 6 servings

tomato salsa

You can throw together this easy salsa in minutes. If you prefer, you can first sauté the pepper and onion.

1 pound ripe tomatoes, diced, or 2 cups canned

½ cup chopped green or yellow bell pepper

½ cup chopped sweet onion

¼ cup chopped fresh cilantro

¼ teaspoon salt

¼ teaspoon freshly ground black pepper

1 clove of garlic, chopped (optional)

In a medium-sized bowl, thoroughly combine all ingedients. Refrigerate for up to 5 days.

Yield: 3 cups

tortilla tale

Although corn is grown and eaten all over the world, if you ask the average American to comment on ethnic dishes made with or from corn, he or she will most likely think of polenta and Mexican corn tortillas, the flat breads made from *masa harina* (see box on page 145). Wheat-flour and cornmeal tortillas are also popular all over the United States. We eat soft tortillas stuffed and rolled for enchiladas, flautas, and quesadillas, and crisp fried tortillas for tacos, tostadas, and nachos. Tortillas can also be pressed into baking dishes and tart pans and baked for 5 minutes to produce a shell not unlike a bland pastry crust or layered with meat and vegetables to make a "lasagna."

Corn is a major ingredient in Tex-Mex, New Mexican, and Hispanic cuisines. Native Americans eat it fresh, dried, and ground as a staple of their diet. The Pennsylvania Dutch turn corn into wonderful relishes and dry large quantities for their stewed corn dishes. Ask Italian-Americans to describe a dish made from cornmeal and they will immediately wax eloquent on polenta (a variation of American cornmeal mush) and cornmeal gnocchi (tiny dumplings). Those of Romanian descent call their corn mush *mamaliga*, which can be eaten as hot cereal or baked or fried like polenta. Whichever way they are served, ethnic cornmeal dishes are considered a staple food, just like bread, pasta, and potatoes.

grits

In the southern United States, hominy (bleached and skinned whole corn kernels, called "posole" in the southwestern states) is eaten daily in the form of grits, a coarsely ground cornmeal. (The term "grits" comes from the Old English word *grytt*, for bran.) Hominy grits are produced from dried yellow or white corn, which is steamed (rather than subjected to the old method of lye treatment) to loosen the hulls. To ensure a long shelf life, commercial grits also have the oily germ removed. The remaining endosperm is cracked between steel rollers and screened to leave behind the largest granules. These are regular hominy grits. To obtain quick grits, the corn is milled into smaller granules. The same process is used to produce cornmeal and corn flour. Medium-sized granules are packaged as cornmeal; the finest granules become corn flour. Grits are served at breakfast along with sausage, ham, and eggs, and they are often topped with butter or gravy.

Grits go back to 1607, when members of the London Company came ashore in Jamestown, Virginia. They were welcomed by the local Native American tribe with bowls of *rokahaměn*, a mush of hot maize. It tasted good to the hungry seafarers and was adopted by their community. They learned to grind it a little finer and called it hominy grits. Since that time, grits have become a mainstay of Southern cuisine, which features grits and gravy, grits and eggs, grits with meat, grits and cheese, grits and sausage, grits and grillades (sautéed or grilled meat with herbs), and other combinations.

Grits are available at most large supermarkets and specialty grocery stores throughout the United States. If you live near a working corn gristmill, you may be able to buy grits and cornmeal with the germ intact.

basic breakfast grits

Grits are a fixture on breakfast menus south of the Mason-Dixon line. Unfortunately, many restaurants serve white grits that have had both the hulls and the germs removed, and the result is a bowl of flavorless mush. I generally don't use salt in my cooking, but it is an essential ingredient in basic breakfast grits.

4½ cups water

1 teaspoon salt

1 cup quick-cooking grits (not instant)

savory or sweet flavorings (see box at right)

1. In a medium-sized saucepan, bring the water to a boil and add the salt.

2. Gradually whisk in the grits.

3. Reduce the heat to medium and, stirring occasionally, cook the grits until they begin to boil and thicken, about 6 minutes.

4. Add savory or sweet flavorings and thin with a drop of water or milk if the mixture is too thick for you.

Yield: 4 servings

sweet and savory grits

A bowl of plain grits is simply mush, but add a little butter, salt, and pepper and it takes on some character. Stir in sharp Cheddar and you really have something tasty. For sweetness, add raisins and chopped nuts or maple syrup and ground cinnamon. Slice or mash a banana and add that, too. Top with some apple slices sautéed in butter and sprinkled with cinnamon and brown sugar. Add savory flavor and bulk with puréed or chopped vegetables and grated cheeses. Or try a little olive oil and fresh herbs or spicy sauces. For brunch, top grits with meat or bean chili. Just think of grits as another staple like potatoes, pasta, and rice.

grits and cheese pudding

I like to serve this dish with a chunky tomato and corn salsa — homemade or prepared, depending on time constraints.

5 cups water

1 cup grits

1 cup grated Cheddar, Muenster or Monterary Jack cheese (a mix of leftover pieces works well)

2 tablespoons butter

1 cup low-fat milk

2 eggs

2 tablespoons snipped fresh chives or scallion greens

½ teaspoon freshly ground black pepper

1. Preheat the oven to 325°F and grease a 1½-quart casserole dish.

2. In a 2-quart saucepan, bring the water to a boil. Slowly add the grits. Return to a boil, reduce the heat, and simmer for 15 minutes, stirring occasionally.

3. Remove from the heat and stir in the cheese and butter.

4. Beat together the milk, eggs, chives, and pepper.

5. Stir the egg mixture into the grits; pour into the casserole.

6. Bake for 40–45 minutes.

Yield: 6–8 servings

Never thrust your own sickle into another's corn.
—PUBLIUS SYRUS, *Maxim 593*

corn custard pudding

This is like a deep-dish quiche without the crust.

2 tablespoons olive or vegetable oil

1 medium red onion, chopped

1 red bell pepper, diced

1½ cups corn (if using canned, drain off the liquid and use it to replace some of the milk)

¾ cup grated Cheddar cheese

½ cup low-fat milk

3 eggs, beaten

½ teaspoon dried basil, or 1 tablespoon chopped fresh basil

¼ teaspoon freshly ground black pepper

1. Preheat the oven to 350°F. Grease a 1½-quart shallow casserole dish or a 9-inch by 2-inch baking dish.

2. Heat the oil in a skillet and add the onion and red pepper. Sauté for 5 minutes.

3. Remove from the heat and place in a medium-sized bowl. Add the corn, Cheddar, milk, eggs, basil, and black pepper.

4. Pour into the prepared casserole and bake for 30 minutes, or until a knife inserted into the center comes out clean.

Yield: 4–6 servings

huevos rancheros

This Mexican-style egg dish is a good way to get out of the usual fried-egg-on-toast routine. For a hearty breakfast, or for brunch, you may want to serve spicy sausages, such as chorizo, on the side. Side dishes of salsa, sour cream, chopped sweet onion, and guacamole will turn this dish into a regular favorite.

1 can (16 ounces) black beans, rinsed and drained

2 cups Tomato Salsa (see recipe on page 25)

four 6- or 8-inch corn tortillas

cooking oil spray

4 extra-large eggs

1 cup grated Monterey Jack cheese

1. In a small saucepan, heat the beans and 1 cup of the salsa over medium heat for 5 minutes.

2. Heat the remaining salsa separately — on top of the stove or in the microwave for 1 minute.

3. Warm the tortillas (see box on page 119).

4. Lightly spray a large non-stick skillet with cooking oil and place over medium heat for 1 minute. Add the eggs to the skillet and cook to desired doneness.

5. Arrange the tortillas on individual plates, top with the black bean mixture, the fried eggs, ¼ cup of the hot tomato salsa, and a spoonful of the grated cheese. Serve the remaining cheese and salsa at the table.

Yield: 4 servings

corn frittata

Frittatas are so versatile. You can make them for yourself from leftover vegetables or fruit. I do this about once a week to use up odds and ends and make a satisfying brunch dish at the same time. Serve with chopped tomatoes and scallions.

2 tablespoons olive or vegetable oil

1 small zucchini, sliced

1 small red bell pepper, diced

1 small onion, chopped

1 clove of garlic, crushed or minced

1½ cups corn kernels (cut from 3 ears of fresh corn)

2 tablespoons chopped fresh basil, or 1 teaspoon dried basil

½ teaspoon coarsely ground black pepper

8 eggs

¼ cup low-fat milk, vegetable juice, or water

1. Preheat the oven to 350°F.

2. Heat the oil in a 10-inch ovenproof skillet.

3. Over medium heat, sauté the zucchini, red pepper, onion, and garlic for 5 minutes.

4. Add the corn, basil, and black pepper and cook 2 minutes longer.

5. In a medium-sized bowl, beat together the eggs and milk. Pour over the vegetables and cover the skillet.

6. Bake for 15 minutes, or until the eggs are cooked to your liking.

Yield: 4 servings

regular cornbread

I don't add salt to most of my recipes. If you want to perk up this plain cornbread, add ½ teaspoon of salt or 4 slices of crispy, crumbled low-fat turkey bacon. I sometimes add 1 cup of corn kernels or ½ cup of grated Cheddar plus ¼ cup of sliced scallions. Use this recipe for the stuffings on pages 96–99.

1 cup yellow cornmeal

1 cup all-purpose flour

1–2 tablespoons sugar

1 tablespoon baking powder

1 cup low-fat milk

2 eggs, beaten

¼ cup olive or vegetable oil or melted butter

1. Preheat the oven to 425°F and grease an 8- or 9-inch-square by 2-inch-deep pan.

2. Combine the cornmeal, flour, sugar, and baking powder in a large mixing bowl.

3. Make a well in the center; pour in the milk, eggs, and oil.

4. Stir until just moistened (the batter will be lumpy), then spoon the batter into the pan.

5. Bake for 20 minutes, or until a toothpick inserted into the center comes out clean.

Yield: 12 servings

traditional cornbreads

All manner of breads can be made from finely ground cornmeal, water, and melted fat. The reason there are so many types of flat cornbreads and cakes is that cornmeal and corn flour contain very little gluten. In other words, they have no leavening power, and the result is a dense texture with no elasticity. Even with the addition of baking powder, cornbreads made exclusively with cornmeal are much flatter and denser than those made with a mixture of cornmeal and flour.

The Hopi Indians make ceremonial breads, such as *chukuviki*, a cornbread wrapped in corn husks and steamed, and *piki*, two paper-thin pancakes rolled together. Corn pone — mounded, oven-baked or fried bread — originated from the Algonquins' bread, *appome* or *apan*. The Narraganset Indians wrapped small mounds of stiff batter in leaves and baked them in hot ashes. These were called ash cakes, or hoe, by the settlers; stick cakes were baked on the end of a long hoe or stick; and johnnycakes were baked beside an open fire. From the Native Americans, the settlers also borrowed Indian or hasty pudding (cornmeal, milk, and spices sweetened with molasses), boiled and fried mushes, corn muffins, corn dodgers (small and extremely dense rounds of batter either baked or fried), and puddinglike spoon bread. For quick-bread variations, use the muffin recipes (pages 47–56) and bake in pans instead of cups. In addition, you can use the quick-bread recipes in this chapter to make muffins.

skillet cornbread

I use a cast-iron skillet for this bread and, though some cooks like to heat the skillet in the oven, I prefer to do it on top of the stove. Try it both ways, but be sure to place the red-hot skillet on top of the stove, not on the counter, while you fill it with batter. A more traditional cornbread is made with bacon fat instead of oil and butter.

¾ cup all-purpose flour

½ cup stone-ground yellow cornmeal

2 tablespoons sugar (optional)

1 teaspoon baking powder

½ teaspoon salt

½ teaspoon freshly ground black pepper

½ cup low-fat milk

1 egg

2 tablespoons olive or vegetable oil

1½ cups corn kernels, fresh, canned, or frozen

1 tablespoon butter

1. Preheat the oven to 450°F.

2. Heat an 8- or 9-inch cast-iron skillet over medium heat.

3. In a large bowl, mix the flour, cornmeal, sugar (if desired), baking powder, salt, and pepper.

4. In a small bowl, beat together the milk, egg, and oil. Stir in the corn.

5. Stir the milk mixture into the flour mixture until evenly combined.

6. Melt the butter in the hot skillet and swish it around the bottom and sides. Pour the batter into the skillet and place it on the middle rack of the oven.

7. Bake for 20 minutes, until the top is golden. Be careful not to overbake.

8. Remove the skillet to a heavy-duty wire rack or place it on top of the stove. Cool for 10 minutes. Invert the skillet onto a cutting board and lift it off. Allow the cornbread to cool 10 minutes longer before cutting it into wedges.

Yield: 8 servings

mexican cornbread

Serve this dish with a bowl of chili and you'll get rave reviews. For an extra-spicy version, use Monterey Jack cheese with jalapeño chiles instead of Cheddar cheese.

1¼ cups all-purpose flour

¾ cup cornmeal

1–2 tablespoons sugar

2 teaspoons baking powder

1 teaspoon baking soda

1 cup grated Cheddar cheese

1 cup corn kernels

½ cup chopped mild green chiles (wear gloves when handling chiles)

½ cup sour cream

¼ cup low-fat milk

¼ cup olive or vegetable oil

1 egg, beaten

1. Preheat the oven to 400°F and grease an 8- or 9-inch-square baking pan.

2. Mix the flour, cornmeal, sugar, baking powder, and baking soda in a large bowl.

3. In a separate bowl, combine the Cheddar, corn, chiles, sour cream, milk, oil, and egg. Stir into the flour mixture until barely moistened. The batter will be lumpy.

4. Pour into the prepared pan and bake for 30 minutes, or until a toothpick inserted into the center comes out clean. Serve warm.

Yield: 6–8 servings

popovers

Basic popover batter is made with eggs, milk, and flour — without baking powder or yeast for leavening. It is the high proportion of liquid in the creamy batter that, when baked at a relatively high heat, creates the steam and releases methane, which causes the popovers to puff up and pop over the tops of the pans. Although many people use muffin cups, there are special popover pans that, because they are tall and narrow, help the batter rise high and form a crusty hat. Popovers are temperamental, and no two cooks will turn out the same product. The batter is sensitive to room temperature and humidity, oven type and temperature, and myriad other variables.

cornmeal popovers

Popovers are always a real treat. These are particularly easy to make and don't take too long to bake.

2 tablespoons vegetable oil

1⅓ cups low-fat milk

½ cup cornmeal

½ cup all-purpose flour

2 eggs, beaten

1. Preheat the oven to 425°F. Grease twelve 6-ounce custard or muffin cups. Pour ½ teaspoon of the oil into each cup. Place the cups on a tray and preheat them in the oven.

2. Beat together the milk, cornmeal, flour, and eggs until smooth.

3. Remove the custard cups from the oven. Fill them halfway with batter.

4. Bake for 30 minutes and serve hot.

Yield: 12 popovers

tea scones

These are delicious with butter and jam. For extra flavor, add raisins; dried cranberries; chopped crystallized ginger; or 1 teaspoon of ground cinnamon, ginger, or allspice. To make savory-flavored scones, substitute ½ cup of grated cheese or chopped walnuts for the dried fruits and use 1 teaspoon each of dried thyme and ground sage instead of the spices. You can also add 1 cup of chopped ham, cooked sausage, corn kernels, or cooked chopped vegetables.

1½ cups all-purpose flour

½ cup plus 1 tablespoon cornmeal

¼ cup sugar

1 tablespoon baking powder

4 tablespoons butter

¾ cup low-fat milk

1. Preheat the oven to 425°F and grease a baking sheet.

2. In a large bowl, combine the flour, the ½ cup of cornmeal, sugar, and baking powder. (If using spices or herbs, add them at this point.)

3. Cut the butter into small pieces and add them to the flour mixture. Using a pastry blender or two knives, work it in until the mixture resembles coarse crumbs. (If using dried fruits or savory additions, add them at this point.)

4. Add the milk; stir with a fork until the dough forms a ball.

5. Turn the dough onto a floured surface and knead gently for about 3 minutes, until the dough is smooth.

6. Form the dough into a ball and flatten it into a 1-inch-thick circle. Cut it into six wedges.

7. Sprinkle the baking sheet with the remaining cornmeal and place the wedges in a loose circle. Bake for 15 minutes, until a toothpick inserted into the center comes out clean. Serve warm.

Yield: 6 servings

anadama molasses yeast rolls

This is one of my favorite yeast bread recipes. It's hearty and flavorful and, because of the no-knead batter method, takes less than 1 hour from mixing bowl to table. Legend has it that anadama bread got its name when a grumpy New Englander, waiting for his bread, said impatiently, "Where is that Anna, damn her?" Others say that the name may be related to the Latin *anadema*, which means "an ornament for the head," possibly the name of a harvest bread made from cornmeal.

1 cup cornmeal

⅓ cup nonfat dry milk

⅓ cup molasses

¼ cup olive or vegetable oil

2 packages (2 tablespoons) active dry yeast

2 cups warm water (110–120°F)

1½ cups all-purpose flour

1½ cups whole wheat flour

1. Preheat the oven to 375°F and grease 18 muffin cups.

2. Place the cornmeal, milk, molasses, oil, and yeast in a large bowl.

3. Add the warm water and beat for 1 minute.

4. In a separate bowl, combine the flours and add 2 cups of the flour mixture to the cornmeal mixture. Beat for 2 minutes with an electric mixer or for 4 minutes by hand.

5. Stir in the remaining flour mixture and beat by hand for 2 minutes. The batter will be sticky.

6. Using a wet or oil-coated spoon, fill the muffin cups with the batter.

7. Cover with a clean cloth, set in a warm place, and let the dough rise for 20 minutes.

8. Bake for 20 minutes, or until a toothpick inserted into the center comes out clean. The rolls will sound hollow when rapped with the knuckles.

9. Remove from the cups and cool on a wire rack. Delicious when served warm.

Yield: 18 rolls

corn kernel yeast bread

I use this as my basic bread recipe. Sometimes I use molasses instead of honey and substitute nuts and raisins for corn kernels and scallions. It's also delicious with 2–4 tablespoons of chopped fresh herbs.

1½ cups corn kernels

⅓ cup nonfat dry milk

¼ cup olive or vegetable oil

¼ cup thinly sliced scallion greens, or 2 tablespoons chopped fresh chives

2 packages (2 tablespoons) active dry yeast

2 tablespoons honey

2 cups warm milk (110–120°F)

1½ cups all-purpose flour

1½ cups whole wheat flour

1. Preheat the oven to 375°F and grease two loaf pans.

2. Place the corn, dry milk, scallions, oil, yeast, and honey in a large bowl.

3. Pour in the warm milk (it should not feel "scalding" to the touch) and beat for 1 minute.

4. In a separate bowl, mix the flours. Beat 1½ cups of the flour mixture into the corn mixture. Beat with an electric mixer for 2 minutes or by hand for 4 minutes.

5. Stir in the remaining flour and beat by hand for 2 minutes. If the batter feels too stiff, add another tablespoon of oil.

6. Using a wet or oil-coated spoon, transfer the batter to the loaf pans, cover them with a clean towel, set in a warm place, and let rise for 20 minutes.

7. Bake for 40 minutes, or until a toothpick inserted into the center comes out clean. The loaves should sound hollow when rapped with the knuckles. Cool on a wire rack.

Yield: 2 loaves

boston brown bread

This is an American classic, though older recipes call for rye flour and require steaming the batter.

1½ cups all-purpose flour, or 1¼ cups rye flour

1 cup whole wheat flour

1 cup cornmeal

2 teaspoons baking powder

1 teaspoon baking soda

2 cups buttermilk

1 cup molasses

2 eggs

1½ cups raisins

1. Preheat the oven to 350°F and grease two 1-pound coffee cans or two loaf pans.

2. Mix the flours, cornmeal, baking powder, and baking soda in a large bowl.

3. In a separate bowl, beat together the buttermilk, molasses, and eggs. Stir in the raisins.

4. Blend the buttermilk mixture with the flour mixture.

5. Spoon the batter into the greased pans and bake for 40 minutes, or until a toothpick inserted into the center comes out clean.

6. Cool 10 minutes in the pan. Remove the loaves and cool on a wire rack.

Yield: 2 loaves

potato-herb batter bread

When I'm not in a hurry, I make this in a 2½-quart casserole dish for the effect of serving a large round loaf. Baked that way, it takes 1 hour in the oven. This bread slices nicely even when warm.

1 cup cornmeal

¾ cup mashed potatoes (don't use leftover mashed potatoes containing milk or other liquid)

¼ cup olive or vegetable oil

2 tablespoons honey

2 packages (2 tablespoons) active dry yeast

1 teaspoon dried basil

1 teaspoon dried oregano

2 cups warm water (100–115°F); use potato water, if desired

1 egg, beaten (optional)

2½ cups all-purpose flour

1. Preheat the oven to 375°F and grease two loaf pans.

2. Place the cornmeal, potatoes, oil, honey, yeast, basil, and oregano in a large mixing bowl.

3. Add the water and beat for 1 minute.

4. Stir in the egg, if desired, and 1½ cups of the flour. Beat with an electric mixer for 2 minutes or by hand for 4 minutes.

5. Beat in the remaining flour by hand for 2 minutes. If the batter feels stiff, add another tablespoon of oil.

6. Using a wet or oil-coated spoon, distribute the batter between the two loaf pans, cover them with a clean towel, set in a warm place, and let rise for 20 minutes.

7. Bake for 40 minutes, or until a toothpick inserted into the center comes out clean. Fully baked loaves will sound hollow when rapped with the knuckles.

8. Remove the bread from the pans and let the loaves cool on a wire rack.

Yield: 2 loaves

cranberry pumpkin bread

This is a lovely tea bread, and the dried cranberries add nuggets of flavor. However, substitute chopped nuts if you don't have dried cranberries; I add them from time to time just for a change. You can also replace the cornmeal with whole wheat flour.

1 cup all-purpose flour

¾ cup cornmeal

½ cup whole wheat flour

⅓ cup firmly packed brown sugar

2 teaspoons baking powder

2 teaspoons ground cinnamon

1 teaspoon baking soda

½ teaspoon ground nutmeg

¼ teaspoon ground cloves

1 cup fresh or canned pumpkin purée

½ cup apple juice

½ cup honey

¼ cup olive or vegetable oil or melted butter

2 eggs

¾ cup dried cranberries or chopped walnuts or pecans

1. Preheat the oven to 350°F and grease a 9- by 5- by 3-inch loaf pan.

2. In a large bowl, combine the all-purpose flour, cornmeal, whole wheat flour, brown sugar, baking powder, cinnamon, baking soda, nutmeg, and cloves.

3. In a separate bowl, beat together the pumpkin, apple juice, honey, oil, and eggs. Stir gently into the flour mixture until barely moistened. The batter will be lumpy.

4. Fold in the cranberries and spoon the batter into the prepared pan.

5. Bake for 50 minutes, or until a toothpick inserted into the center comes out clean.

6. Cool in the pan for 10 minutes. Remove the loaf and cool on a wire rack.

Yield: 8–12 servings

whole corn spoon bread

Serve this dish plain or drizzle it with honey or maple syrup. Vary the flavors by adding 1 cup of sautéed chopped onion, chopped ham, or grated Cheddar cheese or ¼ cup of your favorite fresh herb. Or create a dessert by adding ¼ cup of sugar and 1 teaspoon of ground cinnamon or vanilla extract, or 1 cup of berries, chopped fruit, or nuts.

1½ cups low-fat milk

1 cup buttermilk

1 cup cornmeal

1 cup corn kernels

4 tablespoons unsalted butter

1 tablespoon sugar

½ teaspoon baking soda

3 eggs, separated

1. Preheat the oven to 350°F and grease a 1½- to 2-quart casserole dish.

2. Heat the milk and buttermilk in a large saucepan. When it begins to boil, add the cornmeal slowly in a thin stream; stir until the mixture is thick and smooth.

3. Remove from the heat and stir in the corn kernels, butter, sugar, and baking soda.

4. Beat the egg yolks and stir them into the corn mixture.

5. In a large mixing bowl, beat the egg whites until stiff; gently fold them into the batter.

6. Pour the batter into the casserole and bake for 45 minutes. The spoon bread will be golden brown and puffed like a soufflé. Serve immediately.

Yield: 6–8 servings

spoon bread

Spoon bread originated in the South during Colonial times. It is neither bread nor soufflé but has a consistency somewhere in between. The cornmeal gives the batter a denser texture than a regular soufflé has, and it must be spooned into a dish because it is not firm enough to slice. Without the addition of the corn kernels, it is my favorite form of corn "bread." If it lasts long enough, it *can* be sliced when cold.

berry bread

This cakelike bread is guaranteed to disappear very fast. Serve warm or cool with ice cream or whipped cream. Or turn this recipe into a cupcake recipe and frost it with a mixture of cream cheese and confectioners' sugar.

1 cup cornmeal

1 cup all-purpose flour

⅓ cup sugar

1 tablespoon baking powder

½ teaspoon baking soda

½ cup (1 stick) melted butter

½ cup low-fat raspberry, blueberry, or strawberry yogurt

1 egg

1 cup raspberries, blueberries, or sliced strawberries

1. Preheat the oven to 400°F and grease a square or round 9- by 2-inch-deep baking pan.

2. Mix the cornmeal, flour, sugar, baking powder, and baking soda in a large bowl.

3. In a separate bowl, beat together the butter, yogurt, and egg. Stir into the mixture until just combined. The batter will be lumpy.

4. Gently fold in the berries.

5. Spoon the batter into the greased pan; bake for 25 minutes, or until a toothpick inserted into the center comes out clean.

6. Let cool in the pan for about 5 minutes. Remove and cool on a wire rack.

Yield: 12 servings

Corn, which is the staff of life.

—EDWARD WINSLOW,
Good News from New England, 1624

corn tortillas

A tortilla press makes perfect flat rounds, but if you're not planning to make them regularly, you may want to try this easy hand-rolled method. If you have a 13-inch skillet, you can cook three or four tortillas at one time. Serve the tortillas as bread or stuff them to make enchiladas, flautas, or tacos.

2 cups *masa harina*

1¼ cups warm water

1. In a medium-sized bowl, mix the *masa harina* and water.

2. When the dough begins to form a ball, smooth it with your hands.

3. Divide the dough into 12 equal portions and form them into balls.

4. Place each ball between two sheets of wax paper.

5. Roll out each ball into a 6-inch circle; leave it between the sheets of paper.

6. Continue flattening and rolling until you have a stack of 12 tortillas.

7. Heat a large, heavy cast-iron skillet over medium heat. Remove several tortillas from their wax papers. Without greasing the skillet, fry the tortillas for about 1 minute on each side. They should be soft. Keep them warm (and soft) by wrapping in aluminum foil.

8. Repeat with the remaining tortillas.

Yield: 12 tortillas

taco shells

You can stuff tacos (or pile tostadas) with cooked ground meat; heated leftover chopped chicken; hot or cold crushed kidney or pinto beans; or cold, flaked canned tuna. My standard filling is crumbled veggie-soy or soy burgers heated with Tomato Salsa (see page 25). Drizzle with a spicy salsa, then add layers of grated Cheddar or Monterey Jack cheese, chopped tomatoes, shredded lettuce, and sliced onions. (These also make good fillings for quesadillas with flour tortillas.)

tostadas and nachos

To make tostadas, fry tortillas in a single layer in hot oil for 1½ minutes. Remove with tongs and drain on paper towels. To make nacho chips, cut the tortillas into quarters and follow the same steps. Spread the chips with mashed kidney beans, sprinkle with cheese, and top with chiles or salsa. Pop them under the broiler for 1–2 minutes, microwave on HIGH for 50 seconds, or bake on a baking sheet in a 350°F oven for 5 minutes.

¼ cup vegetable oil

8 corn tortillas

1. Heat the oil in a heavy skillet over medium heat.

2. Place one tortilla at a time in the oil and fry for 20 seconds.

3. Remove the tortilla with blunt-tipped tongs and fold it in half to make a taco shape.

4. Return the tortilla to the hot oil and fry for 30 seconds, keeping the edges apart with the aid of the tongs.

5. Turn and fry until crisp, about 30 seconds. Remove from the oil with tongs and drain on paper towels.

6. Repeat with the remaining tortillas.

Yield: 8 servings

steve coleman's vegetarian muffins

I met Steve Coleman when he was director-naturalist at our local Nature Conservancy sanctuary. He conducted several naturalist training events outdoors, which he made doubly exciting by baking giant, healthful muffins before each session. My favorites included bran and molasses, whole wheat and wild blackberry, and, of course, corn. The following is Steve's basic recipe. He varies the cornmeal with unprocessed bran, rolled oats, or wheat germ (if you do the same, cut the liquid to 1½ cups). He also likes to add nuts, raisins, and fresh fruit.

2 cups whole wheat flour, or
1 cup all-purpose flour and
1 cup whole wheat flour

1 cup yellow cornmeal

2 teaspoons baking powder

1 teaspoon baking soda

1¾ cups fruit juice, soy milk, or water

½ cup honey, barley malt, rice syrup, or molasses

½ cup vegetable oil

1. Preheat the oven to 425°F and grease 8–12 muffin cups, depending on whether you want regular-sized or giant muffins. (For large muffins, completely fill the cups or use 6-ounce custard cups.)

2. In a large bowl, combine the flour, cornmeal, baking powder, and baking soda.

3. In a separate bowl, combine the fruit juice, honey, and oil. Stir into the flour mixture until just moistened. The batter will be lumpy.

4. Spoon the batter into the muffin cups and bake for 20 minutes, or until a toothpick inserted into the center comes out clean.

Yield: 8–12 muffins

four-grain corn muffins

I frequently make this favorite muffin recipe as a bread. It has a crunchy texture and a flavor that makes it ideal for eating on its own (when it's warm, you don't even need butter) for breakfast or as an accompaniment to a savory lunch or dinner.

¾ cup cornmeal

¾ cup all-purpose flour

½ cup Grape Nuts cereal

½ cup rolled oats

½ cup chopped walnuts or pecans

1 tablespoon baking powder

½ cup low-fat milk

¼ cup honey, molasses, or maple syrup

2 eggs

6 tablespoons olive or vegetable oil or melted butter

1. Preheat the oven to 425°F and grease 12 muffin cups or a square or round 9- by 2-inch-deep pan.

2. In a large bowl, combine the cornmeal, flour, Grape Nuts, oats, nuts, and baking powder.

3. In a separate bowl, beat together the milk, honey, eggs, and oil. Combine with the cornmeal mixture until just moistened. The batter will be lumpy.

4. Spoon the batter into the prepared muffin cups and bake for 20 minutes, or until a toothpick inserted into the center comes out clean.

5. Let the muffins cool in the pans on a wire rack; or let the bread cool in the pan for 5 minutes, then remove it and cool on a wire rack or eat warm.

Yield: 12 muffins

cornmeal muffins

These are your basic cornmeal muffins — low on sugar and shortening and containing no vanilla flavoring. They make a superb plain muffin to accompany a savory meal. For a richer and less crumbly muffin, use 4 tablespoons of sugar, 6 tablespoons of oil or butter, and 2 eggs. For Cheese Cornmeal Muffins, simply add ½–¾ cup of grated Cheddar cheese in step 3. Mexican Cornmeal Muffins can be made by adding ½ cup of chopped jalapeño chiles (mild or hot) in step 3.

1 cup yellow cornmeal

1 cup all-purpose flour

3 tablespoons sugar

1 tablespoon baking powder

1 cup low-fat milk

¼ cup olive or vegetable oil or melted butter

1 egg

1. Preheat the oven to 425°F and grease 12 muffin cups or line them with paper cups.

2. In a medium-sized mixing bowl, combine the cornmeal, flour, sugar, and baking powder.

3. In a separate bowl, beat together the milk, oil, and egg. Make a well in the center of the cornmeal mixture and pour in the milk mixture.

4. Stir until just combined. Spoon the batter into the muffin cups and bake for 20 minutes.

Yield: 12 muffins

double corn muffins

Eat one of these hearty muffins for breakfast and you'll sail through the morning.

1 cup cornmeal

1 cup all-purpose flour

1 tablespoon baking powder

½ teaspoon baking soda

¼ teaspoon ground cinnamon

¼ teaspoon ground nutmeg

1 cup corn kernels, fresh, frozen, or canned (drained of all liquid)

1 cup fat-free yogurt

½ cup olive or vegetable oil or melted butter

¼ cup honey

2 eggs

½ cup chopped walnuts (optional)

1. Preheat the oven to 425°F and grease 12 muffin cups or line them with paper cups.

2. Mix the cornmeal, flour, baking powder, baking soda, cinnamon, and nutmeg in a large bowl. Make a well in the center.

3. Place the corn, yogurt, oil, honey, and eggs in a blender and process on MEDIUM for 1 minute. Pour into the center of the cornmeal mixture and stir until just combined.

4. Gently stir in the walnuts, if desired. Leave the batter lumpy.

5. Spoon the batter into the prepared muffin cups, almost filling each one, and bake for 20 minutes, or until a toothpick inserted into the center comes out clean.

Yield: 12 large muffins

blueberry corn muffins

Don't hesitate to use other fresh or frozen fruit in this recipe. Instead of blueberries, substitute 1 cup of cranberries, raspberries, or chopped apples, plums, or peaches. When using a tart fruit, you will probably want to opt for ½ cup of sugar.

1 cup cornmeal

1 cup all-purpose flour

⅓–½ cup sugar

1 tablespoon baking powder

½ teaspoon baking soda

¾ cup low-fat milk

⅓ cup olive or vegetable oil or melted butter

2 eggs

1 cup blueberries

1. Preheat the oven to 425°F and grease 12 muffin cups or line them with paper cups.

2. Mix the cornmeal, flour, sugar, baking powder, and baking soda in a large bowl. Make a well in the center.

3. Beat together the milk, oil, and eggs. Pour the milk mixture into the center of the cornmeal mixture and stir until just combined.

4. Fold in the blueberries without overmixing the batter.

5. Spoon the batter into the muffin cups and bake for 20 minutes, or until a toothpick inserted into the center comes out clean.

Yield: 12 large muffins

muffin cooking tips

When mixing muffins, barely moisten the dry ingredients. A lumpy batter results in more tender muffins. To bake muffins in a microwave oven, use either a special 6-cup microwave muffin pan or six 6-ounce custard cups filled ¾ full; cook uncovered on HIGH for 3 minutes. If your microwave doesn't have a rotating plate, cook on HIGH for 2 minutes, rotate the plate a half-turn, and cook on HIGH 1 minute longer. Microwaved muffins continue to cook after they have been removed from the oven. Their texture is more pudding-like than that of regular muffins. Of course, any muffin recipe can be turned into a quick bread by simply using a square 8- or 9- by 2-inch-deep pan.

molasses apple muffins

Don't hesitate to substitute Granny Smith apples with whatever you have on hand — just don't use Red Delicious apples.

1 cup all-purpose flour

½ cup cornmeal

½ cup whole wheat flour

1 tablespoon baking powder

1 teaspoon ground ginger

½ teaspoon baking soda

½ cup apple juice

½ cup molasses

¼ cup olive or vegetable oil

2 eggs

1 unpeeled Granny Smith apple, cored and grated

1. Preheat the oven to 425°F and grease 12 muffin cups or line them with paper cups.

2. Mix the all-purpose flour, cornmeal, whole wheat flour, baking powder, ginger, and baking soda in a large bowl. Make a well in the center.

3. In a separate bowl, beat together the apple juice, molasses, oil, and eggs. Stir in the apple. Pour this mixture into the center of the flour mixture and combine just until the mixture is lumpy.

4. Spoon the batter into the muffin cups and bake for 15–20 minutes, or until a toothpick inserted into the center comes out clean.

Yield: 12 large muffins

strawberry muffins

If you don't have fresh strawberries, use strawberry preserves or anything else that will provide a delicious surprise.

1 cup white cornmeal

1 cup all-purpose flour

¼ cup sugar

1 tablespoon baking powder

½ teaspoon baking soda
(if using buttermilk)

¾ cup buttermilk or low-fat milk

⅓ cup olive or vegetable oil or melted butter

2 eggs

⅓ cup mashed fresh strawberries or strawberry preserves

1. Preheat the oven to 425°F and grease 12 muffin cups or line them with paper cups.

2. In a large bowl, combine the cornmeal, flour, sugar, baking powder, and baking soda (if using buttermilk). Make a well in the center.

3. Beat together the buttermilk, oil, and eggs. Stir into the cornmeal mixture until just combined.

4. Fill the muffin cups halfway with batter, then add 1 teaspoon of the strawberries in the center. Cover with the remaining batter.

5. Bake for 20 minutes, or until a toothpick inserted into the center comes out clean.

Yield: 12 muffins

spicy whole-grain muffins

These are filled with flavor and nutrition. To reduce the fat content even further, use ½ cup of processed egg substitute or 4 egg whites instead of the 2 whole eggs.

1 cup all-purpose or whole wheat flour

½ cup cornmeal

½ cup raisins

¼ cup bran flakes

¼ cup rolled oats

1 tablespoon baking powder

1½ teaspoons ground cinnamon

½ teaspoon ground ginger

¾ cup low-fat milk

⅓ cup molasses or honey

⅓ cup olive or vegetable oil

2 eggs, or ½ cup processed egg substitute

1. Preheat the oven to 425°F and grease 12 muffin cups or line them with paper cups.

2. Mix the flour, cornmeal, raisins, bran flakes, rolled oats, baking powder, cinnamon, and ginger in a large bowl.

3. In a separate bowl, beat together the milk, molasses, oil, and eggs. Combine with the flour mixture until just moistened. The batter will be lumpy.

4. Spoon the batter into the muffin cups and bake for 15–20 minutes, or until a toothpick inserted into the center comes out clean.

Yield: 12 muffins

carrot nut muffins

If you like, you can substitute zucchini or apple for the carrots. (Add ½ cup of grated Cheddar cheese in step 3 to complement the apple.)

1 cup all-purpose flour

½ cup cornmeal

½ cup whole wheat flour

⅓ cup firmly packed brown sugar

1 tablespoon baking powder

½ teaspoon ground cinnamon

½ teaspoon ground nutmeg

¾ cup low-fat milk

⅓ cup olive or vegetable oil

2 eggs

1 cup grated carrot

½ cup chopped walnuts or pecans

1. Preheat the oven to 425°F and grease 12 muffin cups or line them with paper cups.

2. Combine the all-purpose flour, cornmeal, whole wheat flour, sugar, baking powder, cinnamon, and nutmeg in a large bowl.

3. Beat together the milk, oil, and eggs. Stir in the carrot. Pour into the flour mixture; combine until just moistened.

4. Fold in the walnuts.

5. Spoon the batter into the muffin cups and bake for 20 minutes, or until a toothpick inserted into the center comes out clean.

Yield: 12 large muffins

add-ins

The variations on a basic corn muffin recipe are practically endless. You can pack a lot of nutrition into muffins by adding ½ cup of nuts, chopped fruit or vegetables, cheese, fruit juice, or anything else you and your family enjoy. To vary the flavor of a basic recipe, try adding 1–2 tablespoons of grated orange zest and substituting orange juice for the milk. Add 1 cup of mashed ripe banana or puréed corn kernels, or put a peanut butter surprise in the center of each muffin. It's hard not to go on and on about muffin possibilities. Experiment!

bacon scallion muffins

Turkey bacon makes a good low-fat alternative to pork bacon, so don't hesitate to subsitute.

4 slices bacon

1¼ cups all-purpose flour

¾ cup yellow cornmeal

1 tablespoon baking powder

1 cup low-fat milk

¼ cup olive or vegetable oil

1 egg

1 cup corn kernels

½ cup finely sliced scallions, or ¼ cup chopped chives

1. Preheat the oven to 425°F and grease 12 muffin cups or line them with paper cups.

2. Cook the bacon until brown. Drain on paper towels. When cool, crumble into a bowl.

3. Combine the flour, cornmeal, and baking powder in a large bowl.

4. In a separate bowl, beat together the milk, oil, and egg. Stir in the bacon, corn, and scallions. Pour into the flour mixture and stir until just moistened. The batter should be lumpy.

5. Spoon the batter into the muffin cups and bake for 20 minutes, or until a toothpick inserted into the center comes out clean.

Yield: 12 large muffins

2

SOUPS & SALADS

soups and hearty salads are easy to make, nourishing, delicious, and satisfying to eat. They can be spontaneous affairs made from whatever is on hand. Or you might plan a recipe around them to take advantage of what is growing in the home garden or available at the farmers' market. You can create an entire meal centering on soup and salad.

corn, bean, and squash soup

Native Americans call this trio of staple vegetables the "three sisters."

2 tablespoons olive or vegetable oil

1 large onion, chopped

two 8-inch zucchini, sliced ½ inch thick, or 2 cups peeled and cubed butternut squash or pumpkin

3 cloves of garlic, minced

2 cups vegetable stock or fat-free, low-sodium chicken broth

2 cups cooked or canned pinto or red kidney beans, rinsed and drained

2 cups chopped tomatoes, fresh or canned

1 teaspoon dried basil

1 teaspoon dried oregano

1 teaspoon dried thyme

2 cups corn kernels, fresh, canned and drained, or frozen

1. Heat the oil in a large skillet over medium heat and sauté the onion for 3 minutes, or until softened.

2. Add the zucchini and garlic and cook 5 minutes longer.

3. Add the stock, beans, tomatoes, basil, oregano, and thyme. Simmer 15 minutes longer (25 minutes longer if using butternut squash or pumpkin).

4. Add the corn and cook 10 minutes longer.

Yield: 4–6 servings

corn and shrimp soup

My family thinks this soup is absolutely delicious. For a richer broth, substitute 1 cup of low-fat milk for 1 cup of the stock. Sometimes I also add 1 teaspoon of curry paste.

1 tablespoon olive oil or butter

1 large onion, thinly sliced

3 ears fresh sweet corn, or 1½ cups frozen or canned kernels, drained

2 cups fat-free, low-sodium chicken broth

1 teaspoon fresh thyme leaves

½ teaspoon coarsely ground black pepper

½ teaspoon fresh tarragon leaves

1½ pounds medium shrimps, shelled and deveined

¼ cup chopped fresh chives

1. Heat the oil in a large skillet and add the onion.

2. Sauté for 4–5 minutes over very low heat, until golden.

3. Using a sharp knife and working from the top to the bottom of each ear, remove the corn from the cobs.

4. In a blender or food processor, blend the onion, corn, broth, thyme, pepper, and tarragon until smooth.

5. Pour the mixture into the skillet and heat for 2 minutes, until steaming.

6. Add the shrimps and cook over low heat 2–3 minutes longer.

7. Spoon into bowls and sprinkle with chives.

Yield: 2–4 servings

tofu thai curry soup

One of the easiest soups to make, and also one of the most delicious, this is based on a tofu dish that I eat whenever I visit my local Thai restaurant. Serve it with jasmine rice and peanuts.

1 tablespoon vegetable oil

3 cloves of garlic, finely minced

1 tablespoon red curry paste (this is "American hot," about three stars)

4 cups coconut milk (a light version is available in many supermarkets)

1 tablespoon fish sauce (optional)

2 packages (12 ounces each) extra-firm (not silken) tofu, preferably organic or fresh from a local Asian market, cut into 1-inch cubes

2 cups canned or frozen baby corn or whole corn kernels, drained

1 small canned red chile, finely sliced (wear gloves when handling chiles)

handful fresh Thai basil, cinnamon basil leaves, or any fresh basil leaves or cilantro

1. Heat the oil in a wok over medium heat; add the garlic and sauté until light gold.

2. Add the curry paste to taste, blend, and cook 1 minute.

3. Add the coconut milk and fish sauce, if desired, and mix them into the curry.

4. Add the tofu, corn, and chile and simmer 10 minutes longer. Add the basil.

5. Pour the soup into a heated, covered casserole dish and serve.

Yield: 6 servings

tortilla soup

This soup is a guaranteed winner with both kids and adults. Vary the ingredients to suit what you have on hand — it makes a great vehicle for leftovers.

cooking oil spray

four 6-inch corn tortillas, cut into 6 wedges, or 24 baked tortilla chips

4 cups low-fat, low-sodium chicken broth

1 can (16 ounces) kidney beans, rinsed and drained

1 large red bell pepper, diced

2 cloves of garlic, minced or crushed

½ teaspoon ground cumin

2 cups cubed cooked chicken

2 large ripe tomatoes, cut into chunks, or 1 cup canned stewed tomatoes

1 cup corn kernels, fresh, frozen, or canned and drained

½ cup chopped fresh cilantro

1. Spray a 5-quart stockpot with oil and place it over medium heat.

2. Add the tortillas and cook for 3 minutes, turning occasionally, until crisp and toasted. Remove from heat and drain on paper towels.

3. Add the broth, beans, pepper, garlic, and cumin and bring to a boil. Reduce the heat, cover, and simmer for 5 minutes. Stir in the chicken, tomatoes, and corn and simmer 3 minutes longer, until ingredients are heated through.

4. Place 4 to 6 tortillas at the bottom of individual bowls, spoon soup over them, and sprinkle with cilantro.

Yield: 4–6 servings

tips on freezing soup

Soup in the freezer can be a lifesaver. Make an extra batch with freezing in mind or freeze leftover soup immediately. The flavor and texture remain intact for up to six months when soup is frozen. To make thawing easy, freeze the soup in pint or quart containers with tight-fitting seals (leave ½ inch at the top to allow for expansion in the freezer). When you want to use the soup, take it out of the freezer one day ahead and put it into the refrigerator. If you forget to thaw it overnight, place the container in a bowl of hot water and allow it to thaw around the edges. Slide it into a saucepan, cover, and thaw over low heat. Make sure you heat it through before serving.

CHEF PROFILE: christy velie

Dining on the exciting Nuevo Latino dishes produced by chef Christy Velie at Café Atlántico in Washington, D.C., brings home the realization that there's more to Latin American cuisine than a plate of sizzling steak or a piece of fish accompanied by copious amounts of beans and rice. While there is not a drop of Latin blood in her young veins, Christy is turning out appetizers and entrées dressed in a spectrum of tantalizing flavors. Some of her signature dishes are Chilean sea bass with fiery Salvadoran sausage; duck confit on herb-infused green rice risotto; Argentine rib-eye steak over puréed tropical malaga tuber; and grilled pork chop marinated to a fiery moistness in Jamaican jerk sauce. Her appetizers run the gamut from a sweet purée of plantains with roasted peanuts and shreds of pork confit to a delectably grilled, head-on crusted shrimp with spicy carrot-ginger sauce. And more than 20 appetizer-sized courses, called Latino Dim Sum, are served as lunch on Saturdays by reservation only.

The dishes that make my heart beat faster include a cilantro-flavored corn soup with chive oil (see recipe on the facing page); seviche de camarones of fresh shrimp, corn, and jalapeño chiles (see recipe on page 95); and quesadillas stuffed with corn, sofrito, and *huitlacoche*, or "Mexican truffles" (a parasitic mushroom type of fungus that sometimes develops on ears of corn; see page 146 for recipe and more information).

corn soup with chive oil

Christy Velie of Café Atlántico shared this recipe with me, so now I can prepare it at home. This frees me to choose one of her other delectable offerings when I dine at the restaurant. Epazote, used in this recipe, is a pungent herb also called "Mexican tea" and "wormseed."

1 onion, finely diced

2 tablespoons butter

2 tablespoons olive oil

1 clove of garlic, minced

8 cups fresh yellow corn kernels

4 cups heavy cream

2 cups water

1 bunch fresh cilantro, chopped

5 sprigs fresh epazote or coriander, leaves removed and chopped

salt and freshly ground white pepper

small bunch fresh chives

1 cup corn oil

1. Sauté the onion in the butter and oil over medium heat until soft and translucent. Add the garlic; cook 2 minutes longer.

2. Add the corn and cook 5 minutes longer, until tender.

3. Add the cream, water, cilantro, epazote, and salt and pepper to taste; stir to combine. Bring to a boil, then remove from the heat.

4. Warm a soup tureen or serving bowl. In a food processor or blender, purée the soup in two batches until smooth. Strain through a fine-mesh sieve over the soup tureen. Taste and adjust the seasonings, if needed.

5. Bring a small saucepan of water to a boil. Blanch the chives for 10 seconds.

6. In a food processor or blender, process the chives and ½ cup of the corn oil until smooth. Slowly drizzle the remaining oil through the feed tube until the mixture is smooth. Add salt to taste.

7. Drizzle the chive oil over the soup; serve warm.

Yield: 8–10 servings as an appetizer, 6 as a main course

cold garden vegetable soup

You can make this soup from whatever is available in the garden or at the farmers' market. This thick but light dish can double as a salsa (leave it chunky) or as a sauce for pasta, fish, and polenta dishes.

1 medium-large sweet onion or medium red onion, chopped

2 cloves of elephant garlic, quartered

2 cloves of regular garlic

2 large red or yellow-orange bell peppers, cut into chunks

1 small bunch scallions, cut into 2- to 3-inch lengths (optional)

two 6-inch green zucchini, cut into chunks (optional)

one 8- to 9-inch cucumber, peeled, seeded, and cut into chunks

2 pounds ripe tomatoes, quartered (use a plate to catch the juice)

handful fresh basil or cilantro leaves, or 1 tablespoon fresh tarragon leaves

½ teaspoon salt

½ teaspoon freshly ground black pepper

2–3 ears sugar-enhanced or supersweet corn, husked and kernels scraped from the cob

1. Place the onion and both garlics in a food processor and process into small chunks, about 30 seconds.

2. Add the peppers and scallions, if desired, and process 30 seconds longer.

3. Add the zucchini, if desired, and cucumber and process 20–30 seconds longer.

4. Add the tomatoes, basil, and salt and pepper to taste. Process to a crushed consistency.

5. Add the corn and process 10–20 seconds longer. Or remove the tomato mixture from the processor and stir in the corn.

6. Serve at room temperature or refrigerate.

Note: Vegetable processing time may vary, depending on whether you prefer fine or chunky soup. With a smaller food processor, you may need to do this in two batches.

Yield: About 10 cups

quick corn and bacon chowder

Whenever I have leftover boiled or mashed potatoes, I toss them into soup, fix hash, or fry up potato cakes. In fact, I usually make extra potatoes, so that I'll have leftovers. The same goes for creamed corn. It makes a delicious addition to soufflés, puddings, omelettes, pancakes, muffins, and — of course — chowder.

4 slices bacon

1 tablespoon olive or vegetable oil

1 medium onion, chopped

4 cups low-fat milk

2 cups creamed corn (or use whole cooked or canned corn kernels and process into a chunky purée in a food processor or blender)

2 cups mashed potatoes

1 tablespoon ground coriander

½ teaspoon coarsely ground black pepper

¼ cup chopped fresh dill, cilantro, or parsley leaves

1. Heat a large kettle and cook the bacon until crisp. Remove the slices and drain on paper towels. Discard the fat. When cool, crumble the bacon to use as garnish. Set aside.

2. Add the oil to the kettle and sauté the onion over medium heat until lightly golden, about 4 minutes.

3. Add the milk, corn, potatoes, coriander, and pepper. Cover partially; simmer over low heat for 15 minutes, or until hot.

4. Sprinkle a little dill and bacon on top of each serving.

Yield: 6 servings

chowder combos

Chowders are particularly appealing in summer, when corn is fresh. However, I don't hesitate to make them year-round with canned or frozen corn. For eye-pleasing combinations, serve chowder sprinkled with chopped fresh herbs and side salads of red peppers, spinach, vine-ripened tomatoes, mozzarella, and fresh basil. Place a basket of fresh-baked muffins on the table, and you'll make your family and guests very happy. *Bon appétit!*

corn and red pepper chowder

When a soup contains potatoes and milk, it is usually called a chowder. Chowder comes from the French *chaudière* — a cauldron in which Breton fishermen used to stir up a mess of fish stew.

2 tablespoons olive or vegetable oil

2 leeks, washed and sliced, or 10 scallions, sliced

2 carrots, finely chopped

2 red bell peppers, diced

3 cups chicken stock

2 cups low-fat or regular milk

4 medium red potatoes, peeled, cut into 1-inch cubes

1 bay leaf

1 teaspoon dried thyme

½ teaspoon coarsely ground black pepper

8 ears corn, or 4 cups corn kernels

¼ cup chopped fresh parsley

1. Heat the oil in a 4- to 6-quart Dutch oven. Add the leeks and carrots and sauté over low heat for 5 minutes without browning.

2. Add the bell peppers and sauté 3 minutes longer.

3. Add the stock, milk, potatoes, bay leaf, thyme, and black pepper. Cover partially and simmer for 20 minutes, until the potatoes are tender but not falling apart.

4. Using a sharp knife and working from the top to the bottom of each ear, remove the corn kernels from the cob. Scrape off all the pulp.

5. Using a potato masher, crush about one-third of the cooked vegetables; add the corn and pulp to the pot. Simmer 10 minutes longer.

6. Sprinkle parsley on top of each serving.

Yield: 6 servings

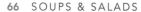

john atwood's curried corn chowder

John Atwood, who has been a regular at my table since 1980, loves to eat, cook, and share recipes. When he gave me this recipe, he said, "The flavors increase as it ages, but it tastes so good you won't be able to resist eating it the first day. So make two batches. It's spicy, so I accompany it with beer, and that's got to be Eagle beer!"

4 medium Idaho baking potatoes, cut into ½-inch cubes

2–4 tablespoons butter

8 large onions, thinly sliced

2 cloves of garlic (optional)

2 tablespoons curry powder

3 cups corn kernels

1 cup light cream

1. Put the potatoes into an 8- to 10-quart Dutch oven and add enough water to come 2 inches above the potatoes.

2. Bring to a boil, then simmer for 15 minutes, or until almost tender.

3. Heat the butter in a large cast-iron skillet and add the onions and garlic, if desired. Cook gently for 5 minutes.

4. Add the curry powder and cook 5 minutes longer.

5. Add the onion mixture and the corn to the potatoes. Simmer 30 minutes longer.

6. Add the cream and simmer 10 minutes longer.

Yield: 8 servings

what makes chowder chowder?

Like all soups, chowders were created by simple folks, who used seasonal ingredients to create a nourishing one-pot meal. The popular theory is that chowders were invented in European fishing villages by fishermen who used their catch and a portion of their seafaring rations of salt pork and biscuits. English and French fisherfolk immigrants then brought the recipes to North America.

lobster and corn chowder

You may be able to pick up ready-cooked lobster at your local store. If not, ask them to boil it for you for about 8 minutes.

4 large yellow potatoes, peeled and diced

1 medium red onion, chopped

1 red bell pepper, chopped

2 quarts water

1 pound lobster meat (from two 1¼-pound lobsters), cut into 1-inch chunks (remove the meat from the claws and reserve the empty shells for adding to the broth)

2 cups creamed corn

2 cups whole corn kernels, fresh, frozen, or canned and drained

1 cup light cream

1 cup milk

½ teaspoon salt

½ teaspoon freshly ground black pepper

2 tablespoons chopped fresh cilantro

1. Place the potatoes, onion, and bell pepper in a 5-quart stockpot, pour in the water, cover, and bring to a boil over high heat.

2. Reduce the heat to medium low and simmer for about 25 minutes, until the potatoes are tender.

3. Stir in the empty claw shells, creamed corn, corn kernels, cream, milk, salt, and black pepper, and simmer 15 minutes longer.

4. Remove the claw shells from the pot.

5. Add the lobster meat and simmer 5 minutes longer. Remove from the heat and ladle into individual serving bowls.

6. Garnish each serving with cilantro.

Yield: 6 servings

seafood gumbo

Authentic gumbo is not fast food. It takes time to stir the roux, which — according to those who hail from Louisiana — is an essential step in the recipe. To save time, toast the flour in the oven. Filé, made from ground sassafras leaves, is a flavoring and thickening agent; it can be found in the seasoning section in most supermarkets. Serve the gumbo with crusty bread or spoon it over rice.

¾ cup all-purpose flour

1 tablespoon olive oil

2 stalks of celery, sliced

1 medium sweet onion, chopped

½ green bell pepper, chopped

2 scallions, sliced

2 cloves of garlic, minced or crushed

1½ quarts vegetable broth or fat-free, salt-free chicken broth

½ teaspoon hot sauce, or ¼ teaspoon cayenne pepper

½ teaspoon salt

½ teaspoon freshly ground black pepper

8 ounces frozen okra (optional)

2½ pounds assorted seafood: shelled shrimps, fresh crabmeat, and large container of fresh oysters with juices

½ teaspoon filé powder (optional)

1. Preheat the oven to 400°F.

2. Spread the flour in a 9-inch pie plate; bake for 15–20 minutes, stirring often, until golden brown (do not allow it to burn). Remove the flour from the oven and let cool.

3. Add the oil to a 5-quart stockpot, place over medium heat, and add the celery, onion, bell pepper, scallions, and garlic. Cook, stirring occasionally, for 5 minutes.

4. Stir in the flour, followed by the broth, hot sauce, salt, and black pepper, and bring to a boil.

5. Reduce the heat and simmer uncovered for 30 minutes. Add the okra, if desired, and cook 30 minutes longer, stirring occasionally.

6. Add the seafood and cook 10–15 minutes longer. Stir in the filé powder, if desired, and remove from the heat.

Yield: 6 servings

corn-stuffed tomatoes

This recipe can be served as a hot baked side dish or prepared to the point of baking and served as a cold luncheon salad. When serving cold, you may prefer to blanch the supersweet corn first or use canned kernels.

6 large ripe, firm tomatoes

4 ears corn, or 2 cups corn kernels

1 red bell pepper, finely chopped

⅓ cup chopped chives or scallion greens

2 tablespoons mayonnaise

1 tablespoon chopped fresh dill

½ teaspoon freshly ground black pepper

¼ teaspoon salt

6 tablespoons grated Cheddar cheese

1. If you are serving this dish hot, preheat the oven to 400°F.

2. Remove a ¼-inch slice from the stem ends of the tomatoes and scoop out the seeds with a spoon. Turn the tomato shells upside down and drain them on paper towels.

3. Using a sharp knife and working from the top to the bottom of each ear of corn, cut the kernels from the cob.

4. Place the kernels in a medium-sized mixing bowl and add the bell pepper, chives, mayonnaise, dill, black pepper, and salt. Combine.

5. Stuff the corn mixture into the tomatoes and sprinkle 1 tablespoon of the Cheddar on top of each one.

6. If desired, bake for 15 minutes and serve as a hot side dish, or chill in the refrigerator and serve as a cold salad.

Yield: 6 servings

rice, lentil, and corn salad

I cook several cups of lentils and rice or make a big batch of salad like this one, because I like to have these ingredients on hand to throw into other spur-of-the-moment dishes. I often substitute canned black beans for the lentils in this dish (as with any canned beans, be sure to rinse them to eliminate the excess salt).

1 cup dried lentils (3 cups cooked)

6 cups cold water

1 cup brown rice (3 cups cooked)

¾ cup olive oil

¼ cup seasoned rice vinegar

2 tablespoons dried herb mixture containing dill

1 tablespoon Dijon mustard

4 large cloves of garlic, crushed

3 cups canned whole corn kernels, drained

1 large red bell pepper, finely diced

4 large scallions, including the greens, thinly sliced

½ cup shredded fresh basil leaves

1. Rinse the lentils, drain, and place in a 2-quart saucepan with 4 cups of the water. Bring to a boil, cover, and simmer for 20–30 minutes, until just tender. Remove and drain.

2. Bring the remaining 2 cups of water to a boil and add the rice. Cover the pot and simmer for 20–30 minutes, until the rice is tender and the water has been absorbed.

3. While the rice and lentils are cooking, prepare the dressing. Place the oil, vinegar, herb mixture, mustard, and garlic in a 2-cup screw-top jar and shake vigorously. Set aside.

4. Rinse the cooked rice under cold water and combine with the lentils in a large bowl.

5. Add the corn, pepper, and scallions. Toss the mixture with the dressing. Chill, if desired, or serve at room temperature. When ready to serve, garnish with basil leaves.

Yield: 8–10 servings

tuna and corn salad

Grilled tuna adds a rich flavor and texture to this salad, which makes a great main course on any day. If desired, marinate the tuna in ¼ cup of the sesame dressing for several hours before cooking. Or drizzle 2 tablespoons of olive oil over the uncooked tuna and rub in ½–1 teaspoon of freshly ground black pepper or hot pepper flakes.

1 pound 1-inch-thick tuna steaks

½–¾ cup Sesame-Peanut Dressing (see recipe on facing page)

2 cups baby corn or whole kernels, fresh, frozen and thawed, or canned and drained

1 medium orange or yellow bell pepper, cut into thin strips

1 medium red bell pepper, cut into thin strips

4 scallions, thinly sliced

¼–⅓ pound (two handfuls) fresh young spinach leaves, washed and patted dry

¼ cup toasted sesame seeds

1. Prepare grill for medium heat.

2. Grill the tuna on an oiled grill rack directly over medium heat for 2–3 minutes on each side (for medium) or 4 minutes on each side (for well done). Let cool.

3. Slice the tuna into ½-inch-thick strips, place them in a dish, and drizzle them with ¼ cup of the dressing.

4. Combine the corn, peppers, and scallions and toss with 2–4 tablespoons of the remaining dressing.

5. Layer the spinach leaves on a serving plate, top with the corn and pepper mixture, and arrange the tuna around the edges. Drizzle the remaining sesame dressing over all and sprinkle with the sesame seeds.

Yield: 2–3 servings

sesame-peanut dressing

½ cup olive oil

¼ cup seasoned rice vinegar

2 tablespoons reduced-fat peanut butter, chunky or creamy

2 tablespoons Thai peanut sauce mix or crushed roasted peanuts

2 tablespoons toasted sesame oil

1 tablespoon light soy sauce

1 teaspoon mirin (Japanese sweet rice wine) or sugar

1 teaspoon grated fresh ginger, or ½ teaspoon dried ground ginger

3 cloves of garlic, crushed

Combine all ingredients in a screw-top jar and shake vigorously to blend. Whisk in the peanut butter if it doesn't blend easily.

Yield: 1 cup

lunch ideas

For a protein-enriched salad, keep on hand a variety of canned beans and corn. Or add beans and corn to a cup of leftover cooked rice, barley, tortellini, or small pasta shapes. Even a cold cooked potato can be cut up and added to the mix. Toss in fresh herbs and drizzle with a vinaigrette. One of my favorite lunches is 1 cup each of corn and chickpeas tossed with 1 teaspoon of sesame oil, ½ teaspoon of curry powder, and grated fresh ginger. Another easy lunch is ¼ cup of Black Bean, Corn, and Tomato Salad (see page 75) atop a flour tortilla, with a shot of hot sauce, a dollop of sour cream or a sprinkling of grated cheese, and some chopped fresh cilantro.

corn with zucchini and red bell pepper

This salad could pass for a salsa or a vegetable side dish. I sauté the vegetables for 5 minutes as a change from the routine of eating fresh salads every day. However, this dish also works very well as a raw salad.

1 tablespoon olive or vegetable oil

1 medium red bell pepper, diced

2 small zucchini, finely diced

2 cloves of garlic, crushed or minced

¼ teaspoon salt

¼ teaspoon freshly ground black pepper

1½ cups corn kernels, fresh, frozen, or canned and drained

½ cup sour cream

¼ cup shredded fresh basil leaves or cilantro leaves, or 1 tablespoon fresh thyme leaves

1. Heat the oil in a large skillet and sauté the bell pepper for 1 minute.

2. Add the zucchini, garlic, and salt and black pepper and sauté 2 minutes longer.

3. Add the corn, cover the skillet, and cook 2 minutes longer.

4. Spoon the mixture into a warm serving dish, add the sour cream and basil, and combine. Serve immediately or chill.

Yield: 4 servings

black bean, corn, and tomato salad

Also a salsa in disguise, this salad is simply wonderful when made with fresh sugar-sweet corn and vine-ripened tomatoes. It is good year-round with frozen corn and canned tomatoes too. I like to roast the (thawed) frozen corn in a dry skillet for about 5 minutes to give it a nutty flavor. Serve the salad on a bed of shredded romaine lettuce, toss it with cooked rice or pasta, or layer it over refried beans and top it with guacamole and sour cream. Or serve the salad as a salsa to accompany fish, meat, or poultry or with tortilla chips as a dip.

4 large ripe tomatoes, chopped (2 cups canned)

2 cups whole kernel corn, fresh or frozen

1 can (15 ounces) black beans or kidney beans, rinsed and drained

1 medium green or red bell pepper, diced

½ cup shredded fresh basil or cilantro leaves

2 tablespoons balsamic vinegar

2 tablespoons olive oil

3 cloves of garlic, crushed

½ teaspoon freshly ground black pepper

¼–½ teaspoon crushed dried red pepper or hot sauce

1. In a large bowl, combine the tomatoes, corn, beans, bell pepper, and basil.

2. Combine the vinegar, oil, garlic, black pepper, and red pepper to taste in a screw-top jar, shake vigorously, and stir into the tomato mixture.

3. Cover the bowl with plastic wrap and chill for at least 2 hours. The flavors will be even better after several hours.

Yield: 6 servings

grilled warm tofu salad

Tofu is delicious with grilled vegetables. For a change, substitute boneless chicken breast for the tofu. When placing sliced vegetables or thin or small foods on the grill, put them in a wire grill basket to make handling and turning easier.

2 packages extra-firm tofu (not silken), packed in water

1 cup Sesame-Ginger Marinade (see recipe at right)

1 large red bell pepper, cut into 1-inch-wide slices

1 orange bell pepper, cut into 1-inch-wide slices

2–3 tablespoons olive oil

2 Japanese eggplants, cut into ½-inch-thick slices

1 pound mixed spring greens or baby spinach

1½ cups baby corn

1. Prepare grill for medium heat.

2. Blot tofu with paper towels. Cut into four ½-inch-thick slices. Put in a baking dish; cover with ½ cup of marinade.

3. In a bowl, toss the peppers with some of the oil. Brush both sides of the eggplant slices with the remaining oil.

4. Arrange the pepper, eggplant, and tofu on a wire rack on the grill and position it directly over medium heat, about 4 inches from the coals. Grill for 7 minutes on each side (brush with oil or marinade when turning), until lightly charred but not burned.

5. Place the greens on a serving plate; top with warm vegetables and corn. Slice the tofu into strips and arrange around the vegetables. Drizzle with the remaining marinade. Serve hot or at room temperature. Pass remaining marinade on the side.

Yield: 4–6 servings

sesame-ginger marinade

½ cup apple juice

½ cup honey teriyaki sauce

¼ cup fresh lime juice

2 tablespoons chopped fresh Thai, cinnamon, or Italian basil

2 tablespoons sesame oil

1 tablespoon chopped fresh mint

3 cloves of garlic, minced

2-inch piece fresh ginger root, grated

Combine all ingredients in a screw-top jar and shake vigorously to blend.

Yield: 1½ cups

barley salad with citrus dressing

Barley has a lovely nutty flavor and makes an interesting alternative to rice. The most common packaged barley is called pearl barley, indicating that it has been refined — the tough hull has been removed, leaving the "pearl" center of the grain. Quick-cooking barley is precooked pearl barley. Regular pearl barley is cooked the same way as quick-cooking barley but takes 30 minutes longer. Whole-grain barley is the complete grain; it contains the most nutrients and fiber but is tough and must be soaked overnight before cooking.

1 tablespoon olive oil

½ cup quick-cooking barley

3 cloves of garlic, minced

1½ cups low-salt vegetable or chicken broth

½ teaspoon salt

½ teaspoon freshly ground black pepper

1 can (16 ounces) chickpeas, rinsed and drained

1½ cups corn kernels

1 cup sliced black olives

½ cup thinly sliced celery

¼ cup chopped fresh parsley

¾ cup Citrus Dressing (see recipe at right)

1. Heat the oil in a large skillet, add the barley and garlic, and sauté for 5 minutes.

2. Add the broth, salt, and pepper. Cover and simmer for 10 minutes, until the barley is chewy and tender. Drain and place in a serving bowl.

3. Add the chickpeas, corn, olives, celery, and parsley and toss to combine.

4. Toss the barley mixture in the dressing (or drizzle on individual servings). Serve immediately or cover with plastic wrap and chill.

Yield: 8 side-dish servings

citrus dressing

½ cup olive oil

juice and grated zest of 2 tangerines or limes

1 tablespoon grated red onion

1 tablespoon ground coriander

½ teaspoon freshly ground black pepper

¼–½ teaspoon ground cumin

Combine all ingredients in a screw-top jar and shake vigorously to blend.

Yield: ¾ cup

roasted garlic

Roasted garlic is mildly pungent and nutty. It adds depth and mellow intensity to salad dressings, sauces, dips, mashed potatoes, and bisques. Spread it on bread — with or without a little olive oil — and you may never go back to eating butter again. There are two ways to roast garlic.

1. Preheat the oven to 350°F. Set 2 whole unpeeled heads (bulbs) of garlic on a large piece of aluminum foil, snip off the tips, and drizzle them with about 1 tablespoon of olive oil. Fold the foil around the garlic bulbs and roast for 45–60 minutes. Allow the bulbs to cool before squeezing the soft roasted cloves from their skins.

2. Preheat the oven to 350°F. Separate the garlic cloves and peel off the skins. Place the cloves in a baking dish, drizzle them with olive oil, apply a few twists from a pepper mill, and sprinkle with ½ teaspoon each of dried or fresh thyme and rosemary, if desired. Cover the dish with foil and bake for 30–45 minutes.

Purée the roasted garlic with about 2 tablespoons of olive oil to make a spreadable smooth paste (it should be neither too thick nor too thin). Two large bulbs plus the olive oil will yield approximately ¼ cup of purée. The salad dressing on the facing page calls for 2 tablespoons of roasted garlic purée; the remaining paste can be refrigerated and added to another batch of salad dressing or used to flavor cream cheese, butter, mayonnaise, mustard, or any kind of dip or spread for breads and crackers.

corn and pasta salad with roasted garlic dressing

Bow ties, small shells, twists, or tortellini — don't hesitate to use any shape of pasta you have on hand. This makes an excellent side dish or appetizer as well.

8 ounces pasta, cooked according to package directions, drained, and rinsed under cold water to chill

2 cups corn kernels

2 large ripe tomatoes, chopped (about 1¼ cups)

1 large orange bell pepper, diced

¾ cup shredded fresh basil leaves

½ cup sliced scallion greens

1 tablespoon minced and seeded jalapeño chile (wear gloves when handling chiles)

¾ cup Roasted Garlic Dressing (see recipe at right)

1 head romaine lettuce

1 cup freshly shaved Parmesan cheese

1. In a large bowl, combine the pasta, corn, tomatoes, pepper, ½ cup of the basil, scallions, and jalapeño. Add the dressing and toss well to combine. Cover and chill, if desired.

2. To serve, bring the salad to room temperature. Line a serving plate with shredded lettuce and spoon salad over the lettuce, or arrange each serving of salad on an individual lettuce leaf. Sprinkle Parmesan and the remaining basil on top.

Yield: 6–8 servings

roasted garlic dressing

½ cup olive oil

2 tablespoons balsamic vinegar

2 tablespoons garlic purée (see Roasted Garlic box on the facing page)

¼ teaspoon salt

¼ teaspoon freshly ground black pepper

Combine all ingredients in a screw-top jar and shake vigorously to blend.

Yield: ¾ cup

foxfire grille's itty bitty crab cakes

FoxFire Grille is a short distance from its sister restaurant, The Red Fox (see recipes on pages 82–83 and 92–93). Located in the Rimfire Lodge in the village of Snowshoe, West Virginia, FoxFire Grille is the place to go for one of the best views of the "rimfire" sunset and for mouth-smacking Southern comfort food. With a name like FoxFire Grille, you'd expect the restaurant to specialize in barbecued meats. And it does. Treated with special dry rubs and smoked over fruitwoods, the barbecues are served with a variety of homemade sauces, some fiery hot. The desserts and salads, like this one, are also something to shout about.

2 tablespoons butter

½ cup minced scallion

¼ cup diced poblano chile (wear gloves when handling chiles)

1 clove of garlic, minced

1 pound lump crabmeat, picked over

1 egg, lightly beaten

¼ cup mayonnaise

2 tablespoons fresh breadcrumbs

2 tablespoons minced fresh cilantro

1 tablespoon Dijon mustard

2 teaspoons minced fresh parsley

1 teaspoon chili powder

1 teaspoon ground cumin

1 teaspoon Old Bay spice

¼ teaspoon salt

¼ teaspoon freshly ground black pepper

2 cups ground or finely crushed tortilla chips

¼ cup cornmeal

½ cup vegetable oil

1 head Bibb lettuce

1¾ cup Jalapeño Tartar Sauce (see recipe on facing page)

1. Melt the butter in a large sauté pan or skillet over medium-high heat and sauté the scallion, chile, and garlic for 1–2 minutes. Remove from the heat; transfer to a bowl.

2. Add the crabmeat and mix thoroughly.

3. In a small bowl, combine the egg, mayonnaise, breadcrumbs, cilantro, mustard, parsley, ½ teaspoon of the chili powder, ½ teaspoon of the cumin, Old Bay spice, salt, and pepper. Gently fold into the crabmeat mixture.

4. Form the mixture into 18 small crab cakes and refrigerate until ready to use.

5. In a medium-sized bowl, mix together the tortilla chips, cornmeal, remaining chili powder, and remaining cumin. Transfer to a large plate or sheet of wax paper. Dredge the crab cakes in the mixture pressing to coat each side evenly.

6. Preheat the oven to 200°F. Heat ¼ cup of the oil in a large sauté pan or skillet over medium-high heat and sauté half of the crab cakes until golden brown on both sides. Drain on paper towels, then put in the oven to keep warm. Heat the remaining oil and sauté the remaining crab cakes.

7. Place a few leaves of lettuce on each of six plates and top each plate with 3 crab cakes. Top each crab cake with 1 tablespoon of the Jalapeño Tartar Sauce. Pass the remaining sauce at the table.

Yield: 6 servings

jalapeño tartar sauce

1 cup mayonnaise

2 tablespoons Dijon mustard

2 tablespoons minced dill pickles

2 tablespoons minced charred (roasted with skin left on) jalapeño chiles (wear gloves when handling chiles)

2 tablespoons minced fresh parsley

1 tablespoon fresh lime juice

1 tablespoon pickle relish

1 tablespoon Tabasco sauce

2 teaspoons ground cumin

1½ teaspoons Worcestershire sauce

1 teaspoon ground coriander

4 cloves of garlic, minced

Combine all ingredients in a small bowl and whisk to blend. Refrigerate until ready to use.

Yield: 1¾ cup

beet and corn salad with ancho buttermilk dressing

The delicious dressing in this recipe complements the sweetness of the beets and corn. Margaret Ann Ball, co-owner and executive chef of The Red Fox restaurant and FoxFire Grille, drizzles it over spring greens for the Cornmeal Oysters with Salsa and Rémoulade (see recipe on pages 92–93). The dressing also pairs well with the New Potato, Corn, and Scallion Salad (see recipe on the facing page).

4 medium beets (1 pound)

¾ cup Red Fox's Ancho Buttermilk Dressing (see recipe on facing page)

8 cups fresh young spinach, arugula, or spring field greens, or one bag (12 to 16 ounces) prewashed baby spinach or greens

2 cups extra-sweet fresh corn or canned corn nibblets, drained

2 ripe (firm) avocados

1. Wash the beets and cut off the leaves and root to within ½ inch of the beetroot. Put into a saucepan and cover with water. Boil, covered, on medium high heat for 45 minutes. Or put into a 9- by 13-inch baking dish, add 2 tablespoons of water, cover with plastic wrap, and micro-wave on HIGH for 20–25 minutes. Let stand 5 minutes before removing plastic wrap.

2. Let cool. Trim the tops and bottoms and slip off the skins (wear plastic kitchen gloves so you don't stain your fingers). Cut into thin slices or ½-inch cubes; toss with ¼ cup of the dressing. Refrigerate until ready to use.

3. Place the greens in a serving dish. Toss with ¼ cup of the remaining dressing.

4. Spoon the corn into the middle of the greens and surround with the beets.

5. Cut the avocados in half and remove the pits and skins. Slice the flesh into ½-inch-thick pieces. Arrange the slices around the outer edges of the salad and drizzle with the remaining dressing.

Yield: 6 servings

the red fox's ancho buttermilk dressing

1 cup buttermilk

⅓ cup sour cream

¼ cup minced fresh cilantro

2 tablespoons minced fresh chives

1 ancho chile, minced (wear gloves when handling chiles)

1 small clove of garlic, minced

½ teaspoon kosher salt

½ teaspoon freshly ground black pepper

Combine all ingredients in a small, deep bowl and whisk to blend. Refrigerate until ready to use.

Yield: 1½ cups

new potato, corn, and scallion salad

I like to make this with new red or white potatoes, which I simply cut in half or leave whole if they are tiny. I also use large yellow, red, or white potatoes or sweet potatoes cut into chunks.

2 pounds tiny new potatoes, scrubbed but not peeled

½ cup low-fat sour cream

½ cup reduced-fat mayonnaise

2 tablespoons lemon or lime juice or white wine vinegar

1 tablespoon coarse-grain mustard

1 tablespoon fresh thyme leaves

4 cloves of garlic, crushed

2 cups corn kernels, fresh, frozen and thawed, or canned and drained

6 scallions, sliced

1. Place the potatoes in a large pan of water, cover, and bring to a boil over high heat. Boil for 12–15 minutes, until tender. Drain and place them in a large bowl. Allow the potatoes to cool slightly.

2. In a medium-sized bowl, combine the sour cream, mayonnaise, lemon juice, mustard, thyme, and garlic. Stir in the corn and scallions.

3. Stir the sour cream mixture into the potatoes, cover with plastic wrap, and refrigerate. Bring to room temperature (about 30–45 minutes) before serving.

Yield: 8 servings

couscous, mango, and corn salad

Couscous is a type of pasta made from the innermost part of durum wheat. I often use whole-wheat couscous, which has more flavor and a chewier texture. The Middle Eastern type of couscous found in specialty stores is twice as large and takes 1 hour to cook. All types of couscous are delicious whether served hot or cold. This salad can become a main dish when topped with sautéed shrimps or scallops, grilled tuna or salmon, or roasted chicken. For the mango, you can substitute a sweet apple, such as Gala, Honeycrisp, Pink Lady, or Crispin.

1½ cups water

½ teaspoon salt

1 cup instant couscous

2 cups fresh extra-sweet corn or canned nibblets, drained

4 large tomatoes, cut into small chunks, or 2 cups diced canned tomatoes

1 ripe mango, peeled and cut into ½-inch cubes

3 tablespoons olive oil

3 tablespoons orange juice

2 tablespoons shredded fresh mint leaves or orange, spearmint, lemon balm, or pineapple salvia leaves

½ teaspoon freshly ground black pepper

1. Place the water and salt in a medium saucepan over high heat and bring to a boil. Stir in the couscous, cover the pan, and remove from the heat. Let stand covered for 5 minutes. Remove to a large bowl and fluff with a fork.

2. Add the corn, tomatoes, mango, oil, juice, mint, and pepper and toss gently to combine. Cover and let stand at room temperature for 30 minutes to blend the flavors or refrigerate until ready to serve.

Yield: 4–6 servings

3

STARTERS
& SIDES

whether you serve simple, savory small dishes at the beginning of a meal or on the side, they round out quick or impromptu meals or enhance a planned dinner. When I invite a crowd, I always include side dishes of pasta, beans, tofu, and salad. That way, I provide a good meal for those who want to eat little or no animal protein.

corn and chickpea hummus

I sometimes make hummus with cannelloni or pinto beans or with half chickpeas and half beans. Vary the flavor by adding hot peppers; curry; or fresh basil, cilantro, or tarragon. Serve as a dip with crackers or spread it on toasted baguette rounds.

2 cans (16 ounces each) chickpeas, rinsed and drained

1 can (11 ounces) white or yellow corn, drained

2 tablespoons reduced-fat mayonnaise

2–4 cloves of garlic

2 scallions, cut into 1-inch pieces (optional)

½ teaspoon hot pepper flakes or freshly ground black pepper or both

¼ teaspoon ground cumin (optional)

¼ teaspoon ground ginger (optional)

1–2 tablespoons olive oil, apple juice, lime juice, or water (optional)

In a food processor, combine the chickpeas, corn, mayonnaise, garlic, scallions (if desired), hot pepper flakes, cumin (if desired), and ginger (if desired); purée until smooth. Add a little oil if desired to create a creamier consistency. Cover and refrigerate until ready to use.

Yield: 3½ cups

ross edwards'
blue blazes hush puppies

I met Ross Edwards years ago when he owned the Blue Corn Connection store in Albuquerque, New Mexico. Although he no longer sells blue corn products, he still makes his famous blue corn hush puppies. Ross serves them with fried fish or alone as an appetizer. Today he buys his blue corn from Jerry Kinsman/Santa Ana Pueblo, on the outskirts of Albuquerque (see Resources, pages 181–83).

½ cup buttermilk

1 egg

1¼ cups blue cornmeal

2 teaspoons baking powder

½ teaspoon salt

½ cup finely chopped green chiles, fresh, frozen and thawed, or canned and drained (wear gloves when handling chiles)

1 small onion, finely chopped

1 large clove of garlic, crushed or minced

¼–½ cup vegetable oil

1. In a medium-sized mixing bowl, beat together the buttermilk and the egg.

2. Stir in the cornmeal, baking powder, and salt.

3. Add the chiles, onion, and garlic. If using thawed or canned chiles, drain very well; if the batter is too wet, add 1 extra tablespoon of cornmeal.

4. Heat the oil in a skillet (it should be about 1 inch deep) and drop the batter in by the teaspoon.

5. Cook 1 minute on each side, until brown and crispy.

Yield: 35 hush puppies

baked layered bean-corn dip

Always a huge hit, this dip is perfect for buffet parties or potluck suppers. Serve it with plenty of low-fat tortilla chips, as well as celery sticks and sliced bell peppers.

cooking oil spray

2 cans (16 ounces each) black beans, rinsed, drained, and mashed, or vegetarian refried beans

1 cup fat-free or low-fat sour cream

1½–2 cups grated low-fat mixed cheeses

1 can (11 ounces) corn kernels, drained

2 cups medium spicy salsa

1 can (6 ounces) sliced chiles in adobo sauce (optional) (wear gloves when handling chiles)

1. Preheat the oven to 400° F. Lightly spray a 9- by 2-inch-deep pie plate with cooking oil.

2. Spread the beans over the bottom of the dish, top with half of the sour cream, and sprinkle with half of the cheese.

3. Spoon the corn and salsa on top. If you are not using chiles, reserve ½ cup of the salsa for the final layer. Spread on the remaining sour cream.

4. Top with the remaining cheese and the chiles, if desired.

5. Cover with foil and bake for 20 minutes. Remove the foil and bake 10 minutes longer.

Yield: 12 servings

avocado, corn, and poblano salsa

This dish can be made with fresh, frozen, or canned corn and chiles. (If using frozen or canned corn, follow the recipe for Pan-Roasted Corn Kernels on page 109.) As a side dish, serve it on a bed of lettuce as an accompaniment to fish. As a starter, serve it atop corn waffles, corn pancakes, or wedges of baked sweet potato.

2 tablespoons olive oil

6 ears corn, husked and silks removed

2 poblano chiles, or 2 medium red bell peppers (wear gloves when handling chiles)

1 medium sweet onion, halved

¼ cup chopped fresh cilantro or cinnamon basil leaves

2 tablespoons lime juice

2 tablespoons orange juice

1 teaspoon grated orange zest (first wash the orange)

¼ teaspoon salt

¼ teaspoon freshly ground black pepper

2 large or 4 small avocados

1. Rub some of the oil over the corn, chiles, and onion.

2. Place a grill rack directly above medium-high heat. Place the vegetables on the rack; cover and grill for 10 minutes, turning two or three times, until lightly charred.

3. Cut the kernels off the cobs, coarsely chop the onion, and place the corn and onion in a medium-sized bowl.

4. Remove the stems and seeds from the chiles, dice them, and add them to the bowl.

5. In a screw-top jar, combine the remaining olive oil with the cilantro, lime juice, orange juice, orange zest, salt, and pepper. Shake vigorously and pour the mixture over the vegetables.

6. Remove the pits and skins from the avocados, cut into ½-inch cubes, and add them to the bowl. Toss all ingredients together. Refrigerate or leave at room temperature for 1 hour for the flavors to meld.

Yield: 8 servings

tuna and corn roll-up appetizer

I make roll-ups pretty much the way I make quesadillas, which means the spreads and fillings vary with whatever I have on hand or can quickly whip together in 5 minutes. I love to use sweet potatoes (I cook them in the microwave) mashed with a little sour cream, olive tapenade, sesame-peanut butter, or hummus (see Corn and Chickpea Hummus on page 86).

six 8- to 10-inch flour tortillas

6 tablespoons soft herb cheese, hummus, or tofu spread

1 can (10 ounces) solid white tuna in spring water, drained and flaked

½ cup canned sweet corn with small kernels, drained

3–4 tablespoons fat-reduced mayonnaise

2 scallions, finely sliced

½ teaspoon freshly ground black pepper

1. Spread each tortilla with 1 tablespoon of the cheese.

2. Thoroughly combine the tuna, corn, mayonnaise, scallions, and pepper.

3. Spoon equal amounts of the tuna mixture on top of each tortilla and spread to within ½ inch of the edges. Starting from the front edge, roll up the tortillas neatly and cut each one in half or thirds.

Yield: 12–18 roll-ups

baked tomatoes with corn custard

Kate Zurschmeide of Great Country Farms in Bluemont, Virginia (see page 160), says this is a versatile recipe that works equally well as a starter or a side dish. It also makes a good dish to serve for brunch or a light supper accompanied by salad greens and bread or muffins.

cooking oil spray

6 firm medium-large tomatoes

1 tablespoon butter

2 tablespoons finely chopped onion

2 tablespoons finely diced red bell pepper

1 egg

¼ cup light cream

2 cups cooked corn or canned corn, drained

¼ teaspoon salt

¼ teaspoon freshly ground black pepper

3–4 tablespoons grated Cheddar or Parmesan cheese

1. Preheat the oven to 400°F and lightly spray a baking sheet with cooking oil.

2. Cut the tops off the tomatoes, scoop out the seeds and pulp, and turn them upside down on paper towels to drain.

3. Melt the butter in a small skillet over medium heat, add the onion and bell pepper, and sauté for 2 minutes.

4. In a medium bowl, beat the egg and cream together, then stir in the corn, onion mixture, salt, and pepper.

5. Spoon the mixture into the tomatoes and sprinkle the tops with the cheese.

6. Arrange the tomatoes on the baking sheet and bake for 15 minutes, until the cheese has melted and the filling has set.

Yield: 6 servings

the red fox's cornmeal oysters with salsa and rémoulade

The Red Fox restaurant is located on the 4,800-foot-high spruce-lined ridges of Snowshoe Mountain in Pocahontas County, West Virginia. Owned and operated by Brian and Margaret Ann Ball, this alpine hideaway houses a trio of restaurants offering fine cuisine and a wine list that has won awards from *Wine Spectator* magazine. Try this recipe and you'll understand why *Fodor's Travel Guide* lists The Red Fox as one of its 25 favorite restaurants in the United States.

1 cup cornmeal

1 cup all-purpose flour

1 teaspoon ground cumin

1 teaspoon salt

½ teaspoon chili powder

½ teaspoon garlic powder

½ teaspoon onion powder

½ teaspoon paprika

½ teaspoon white pepper

1 cup vegetable oil

30 select oysters

six 8-inch corn tortillas, crisped in a warm oven (The Red Fox uses tortilla "bowls")

9 cups spring green mix tossed with Ancho Buttermilk Dressing (see page 83)

3 cups Corn and Black Bean Salsa (see recipe on facing page)

6 teaspoons Poblano Rémoulade (see recipe on facing page)

1. In a medium-sized bowl, combine the cornmeal, flour, cumin, salt, chili powder, garlic powder, onion powder, paprika, and pepper. Pour onto a plate or a sheet of wax paper.

2. Heat the oil in a deep sauté pan over very high heat. Dredge the oysters in the cornmeal mixture. When the oil is spitting hot, deep-fry the oysters for about 1 minute, until golden brown. Remove immediately and drain on two thicknesses of paper towels.

3. Place a tortilla on each plate, pile each with 1½ cups of the spring greens, and top with ½ cup of the salsa.

4. Arrange 5 oysters around the salsa on each serving and top each one with 1 teaspoon of the rémoulade.

Yield: 6 servings

poblano rémoulade

½ cup mayonnaise

¼ cup finely chopped fresh cilantro

1 small poblano chile, minced (wear gloves when handling chiles)

1 tablespoon fresh lime juice

1 teaspoon ground cumin

½ teaspoon kosher salt

½ teaspoon freshly ground black pepper

In a small bowl, thoroughly combine all ingredients. Cover; refrigerate until ready to use.

Yield: ¾ cup

corn and black bean salsa

1 cup black beans, rinsed, drained, and cooked

1 cup fresh corn kernels, lightly steamed and removed from the cob

½ cup chopped plum tomatoes

¼ cup chopped fresh cilantro

¼ cup chopped poblano chiles (wear gloves when handling chiles)

¼ cup chopped red bell pepper

¼ cup chopped scallions

1 tablespoon balsamic vinegar

1 tablespoon fresh lime juice

1 tablespoon olive oil

1½ teaspoons ground cumin

1 teaspoon ground coriander

½ teaspoon kosher salt

½ teaspoon freshly ground black pepper

1 clove of garlic, minced

In a small bowl, thoroughly combine all ingredients. Cover; refrigerate or leave at room temperature until ready to use.

Yield: 3 cups

corn-stuffed belgian endive

Belgian endive leaves are perfectly shaped to hold a light stuffing. Hearts of romaine lettuce, red radicchio leaves, or avocado or pear halves make excellent substitutes.

½ cup reduced-fat mayonnaise

½ cup reduced-fat sour cream

2 cloves of garlic, crushed

2 tablespoons chopped fresh parsley

2 tablespoons chopped fresh chives or scallion greens

½ teaspoon freshly ground black pepper

1 cup corn kernels, fresh cooked, frozen and thawed, or canned and drained

1 cup frozen tender small peas, thawed

8 large leaves Belgian endive

¼ cup finely diced sweet or hot red pepper

1. In a medium-sized bowl, combine the mayonnaise, sour cream, garlic, parsley, chives, and black pepper. Stir in the corn and peas.

2. Spoon the mixture onto the endive leaves, sprinkle with the bell pepper, and serve.

Yield: 8 servings (or 3 cups filling)

shrimp seviche with corn

Made by Christy Velie, head chef at Café Atlantico (see page 62), this dish gets rave reviews. The raw shrimps are "cooked" by the lime juice during marination, and they are superbly tender and flavorful. In the home kitchen, scallops, squid, and octopus make good raw marinated additions or substitutes. Serve with corn chips, corn nuts, or boiled sweet potato.

1 pound fresh shrimps, peeled, deveined, and cut into thirds

6 cups fresh lime juice

1 cup fresh corn kernels, steamed for 1–2 minutes and cooled

1 small red onion, finely diced (about ½ cup)

1 bunch fresh cilantro leaves, chopped

3 tablespoons finely diced celery heart

2 jalapeño chiles, seeds removed and finely diced (wear gloves when handling chiles)

1 teaspoon minced garlic

salt

1. Cover the shrimps with the lime juice and marinate for 3 hours.

2. Strain the shrimps and discard the juice.

3. Combine the shrimps with the corn, onion, cilantro, celery, chiles, garlic, and salt to taste.

Note: Eating raw or partially cooked foods, including marinated fish, may pose a health risk, especially to the elderly, young children, pregnant women, and those with medical problems that may have compromised their immune systems.

Yield: 4 servings as an appetizer, 2 servings as an entrée

whole corn stuffing

This amount of stuffing will fill the cavity of a 7- to 8-pound chicken or a small turkey. Spoon the filling into the cavity, making sure it is loosely packed. Heat any remaining stuffing in a baking dish to serve on the side.

9 slices nutty whole-wheat bread, or 3 cups packaged stuffing mix

2 tablespoons olive or vegetable oil

1 medium onion, chopped

1 red bell pepper, chopped

1 clove of garlic, crushed

1 cup corn kernels

1 can (7 ounces) green chiles, chopped (optional) (wear gloves when handling chiles)

2 teaspoons dried oregano

2 teaspoons dried thyme

½ teaspoon salt

½ teaspoon freshly ground black pepper

⅓–½ cup vegetable or low-sodium chicken broth or apple juice

cooking oil spray

1. Preheat the oven to 350°F. Put the bread on a baking sheet and bake for 15 minutes, until lightly toasted. Crumble or break it into small chunks. Set aside.

2. Heat the oil in a large skillet and add the onion, pepper, and garlic. Sauté for 5 minutes.

3. Add the corn and chiles, if desired; sauté 2 minutes longer.

4. Add the bread to the skillet.

5. Sprinkle with the oregano, thyme, salt, and pepper, then stir in the broth.

6. When using as a side dish, spray a 2½-quart baking dish with oil, add the stuffing, cover with foil, and bake for 30 minutes. Remove the foil and bake 15 minutes longer.

Yield: 6–8 servings

stuffing

Most stuffings are made from a combination of dried bread, sautéed onions and celery, herb seasonings, and vegetable or chicken broth. That basic recipe, of course, is just the beginning of what can become a sublime dish enhanced by sausage, chicken livers, oysters, mushrooms, nuts, fruits, or sweet corn. For example, fruit stuffings made with dried prunes or apricots or freshly chopped apples are particularly delicious with goose or duck. Stuffings made with nuts, sausage, and cornbread are more suited to turkey and chicken. Whole corn, though, can be added to many kinds of stuffings to add a little sweetness without greatly changing the flavor.

You don't need to wait until you roast a whole bird to make stuffing. It makes a hearty side dish for baked chicken, sautéed slices of thick ham, sausages, pork roast, and venison. When stuffed into mushrooms, acorn or butternut squash, eggplant boats, tomatoes, or bell peppers, stuffing adds flavor and nutrition to starters, side dishes, and vegetarian entrées. To prepare vegetables for stuffing, cut the tops off tomatoes and bell peppers or cut squash in half. Hollow out tomatoes (see page 91), remove the seeds from bell peppers and squash, and remove the stems from large mushrooms. Place the vegetables in a baking dish, spoon the stuffing into their centers, and pour ¼ to ½ cup of vegetable or chicken broth or wine into the dish. Loosely cover with foil and bake at 350°F for 15 minutes. Remove the foil and continue baking until the vegetables are tender. This may take 15 to 30 minutes longer for the squash. For instructions on how to bake the stuffing directly inside poultry cavities, refer to the recipe for Ginger-Basted Roast Chicken with Whole Corn Stuffing on page 120.

sausage, mushroom, and corn stuffing

Prepare or buy a classic bread and onion stuffing, add 1 pound of sausage, a little corn, and some fresh sage, then wait for the compliments.

1 pound sweet or spicy sausage, removed from the casings

2 stalks of celery, chopped

1 medium onion, chopped

2–3 tablespoons olive oil

2 cups sliced cremini mushrooms

3 cups cubed bread stuffing

1 cup corn kernels

¼ cup chopped fresh sage leaves, or 1 tablespoon mixed dried herbs

½ teaspoon salt

½ teaspoon freshly ground black pepper

1½–2 cups vegetable broth or fat-free, reduced-salt chicken broth

cooking oil spray

1. Preheat the oven to 350°F.

2. Crumble the sausage into a large skillet and cook over medium heat for 5 minutes.

3. Stir in the celery, onion, and 1 tablespoon of the oil. Cook until vegetables are wilted, about 5 minutes.

4. Add the remaining oil and the mushrooms, stir, and cook 5 minutes longer.

5. Add the stuffing, corn, sage, salt, pepper, and 1 cup of the broth. Gradually stir in the rest of the broth until the stuffing is moist.

6. Spray a 2½-quart baking dish with oil and spoon the stuffing into the dish. Cover with foil and bake for 30 minutes. Remove the foil and bake 15 minutes longer.

Yield: 12–14 servings

pecan cornbread stuffing

Serve this recipe as a side dish or stuff it into the crop and cavity of a 10- to 12-pound turkey and roast 3½ hours in an oven preheated to 350°F. This is also a delicious stuffing for acorn squash and portobello mushrooms.

3 tablespoons olive or vegetable oil

6 large scallions, including greens, thinly sliced

1 red bell pepper, finely chopped

1 cup chopped pecans or walnuts

½ cup chopped fresh flat parsley

1 tablespoon dried mixed herbs ("all purpose")

½ teaspoon salt

½ teaspoon freshly ground black pepper

1 recipe Regular Cornbread (see page 32), crumbled

⅓–½ cup apple juice or vegetable broth

cooking oil spray

1. Preheat the oven to 350°F.

2. Heat the oil in a large skillet and sauté the scallions and bell pepper for 5 minutes.

3. Remove the skillet from the heat and stir in the pecans, parsley, herbs, salt, and pepper.

4. Add the cornbread to the pecan mixture. Stir to combine.

5. Add the apple juice to moisten the stuffing.

6. Spray a 2½-quart baking dish with oil and spoon the stuffing into the dish. Cover with foil and bake for 30 minutes. Remove the foil and bake 15 minutes longer.

Yield: 12 servings

stuffing safety

To avoid contamination from raw juices, stuffing should not be spooned into poultry and then refrigerated before going into the oven. The center of the cold stuffing will not heat sufficiently to kill any bacteria that may be present. Stuff the chicken or turkey right before it goes into the oven to avoid this problem.

fresh corn relish

This a very simple relish to prepare — it goes together quickly because there are so few ingredients to chop. And it's wonderful to open a jar of summer in the middle of winter. If you don't want to fuss with a boiling-water-bath canner, you can make a really quick, uncooked corn relish from the recipe on the facing page.

12 ears corn

1 large onion, finely chopped

1 large green bell pepper, diced

1 large red bell pepper, diced

1½ cups apple cider vinegar

1 cup sugar

¼ cup water

1 tablespoon sea salt

1 teaspoon celery seed

1 teaspoon curry or chili powder (optional)

1 teaspoon dry mustard

1. Using a sharp knife and working from the top to the bottom of each ear, remove the kernels from the cobs. (There will be about 6 cups of kernels and liquid.) Place in a large enamel or stainless steel kettle.

2. Add the onion, green bell pepper, red bell pepper, vinegar, sugar, water, salt, celery seed, curry powder (if desired), and mustard; stir to combine.

3. Bring to a boil, lower the heat, and simmer for 15 minutes. Turn off the heat.

4. With the help of a wide-mouthed funnel, spoon the mixture into hot sterilized canning jars, leaving a ½-inch space at the top.

5. Wipe the jar rims and cover with sterilized lids. Screw down the lids tightly.

6. Place the jars, not touching, in a boiling-water-bath canner and cover with hot water. Bring to a boil and process for 10 minutes according to the manufacturer's instructions. Adjust for altitude, if necessary. Remove from the water with canning tongs and let cool.

Yield: 5 pints

corn herb relish

No cooking is involved with this quick and easy relish, so eat it or store it in the refrigerator for up to 2 weeks. Serve with fish or chicken.

1 cup corn kernels, fresh, frozen, or canned and drained

1 medium red bell pepper, finely chopped

½ small red onion, finely chopped

2 tablespoons lime juice

2 tablespoons chopped fresh spearmint

1 tablespoon seasoned rice vinegar

1 teaspoon mirin (Japanese sweet rice wine) or superfine sugar

1 jalapeño chile, seeded and finely chopped (wear gloves when handling chiles)

1 clove of garlic, minced

½ cup sour cream (optional)

In a small bowl, thoroughly combine all ingredients. Cover and refrigerate until ready to use.

Yield: 2 cups

relishes

Pennsylvania Dutch country is famous for its corn relish and sweet-and-sour chow-chow pickles. The chow-chow, made from as many as 14 vegetables, including corn, is so thick that it is often served as a side dish. Many relishes are cooked briefly, bottled, and then processed in a boiling-water bath. If you aren't putting up vast quantities and shelf life isn't a concern, you can get away with making a quick refrigerator relish. Most relishes made today are more like salads and are packed with lovely fresh flavors. If it's a disadvantage that they must be eaten within a week or two, I haven't noticed it. In fact, they are so delicious that they don't hang around our house for more than two or three days.

calabacitas with corn and squash

This casserole is adapted from a class I took at the Santa Fe School of Cooking in New Mexico (see the facing page). Susan Curtis, owner of the school, says that in many Santa Fe homes, *calabacitas* — a traditional dish of the Pueblo Indians of the Southwest — is made as a one-dish casserole by baking it and adding chicken or beef. This one is vegetarian and cooks on top of the stove in 20 minutes.

3–4 tablespoons olive oil

1 cup finely chopped onion

2–4 cloves of garlic, minced

2½ cups diced summer squash

2½ cups diced zucchini

2 cups corn kernels, fresh or frozen

6 scallions, chopped (¾ cup)

½ cup chopped hot green chile, roasted, with skin removed (wear gloves when handling chiles)

½ cup chopped mild green chile, roasted, with skin removed

1 cup diced ripe Roma (plum) tomatoes

½ cup firmly packed coarsely chopped fresh cilantro leaves

½ cup cream or grated Jack cheese (optional)

½ teaspoon salt

1. Heat 2 tablespoons of the oil in a large skillet and sauté the onion for about 4 minutes over medium-high heat. Add the garlic and sauté 2 minutes longer.

2. Add the squash and zucchini and sauté 5 minutes longer, until softened.

3. Add the remaining 1 to 2 tablespoons of oil with the corn, scallions, and chiles and sauté 3 minutes longer.

4. Stir in the tomatoes, cilantro, and cream (if desired) and heat through, about 5 minutes.

5. Season with salt. Serve hot or warm.

Yield: 8–10 servings

santa fe school of cooking

The soul of Santa Fe cooking is powered by the many varieties of chile peppers and corn that find their way, in one form or another, into most of the dishes prepared in New Mexican kitchens. A great way to learn about authentic New Mexican foods is to take a course at the Santa Fe School of Cooking. Director Susan Curtis founded the school in 1989 as a way to showcase the native cuisine and culture of the Southwest. The author of several cookbooks on Southwestern cuisine, Curtis shares her knowledge of the region during four-day culinary and cultural tours through northern New Mexican villages. The culmination of the trip is a cooking class on the foods of the Southwest Indian nations.

I took classes featuring northern New Mexican dishes, such as *posole* (see page 149), *chiles rellenos*, *calabacitas* (see the facing page), *carne adovada*, and blue corn and green chile muffins. In contemporary Southwestern cuisine classes, the dishes are built around traditional ingredients, but the recipes are given a modern twist; some examples include Lime-Marinated Grilled Salmon with Corn, Tomatoes, and Black Bean Salsa (see recipe on pages 152–153) and Blue Cornmeal Shortcakes and Berries (see recipe on page 166). Other classes tempting my return to the school include Southwest and New World Tapas, Southwest Vegetarian, and Cuisines of Mexico, all of which feature recipes made with some of my favorite foods — corn, black beans, chile peppers, shrimp, goat cheese, cilantro, tomatoes, tortillas, breads, and more. For more information on the Santa Fe School of Cooking and its market, which features regional foods and cooking equipment, see Resources on page 183.

corn and snap pea succotash

Succotash is a traditional Native American dish. This recipe celebrates the summer-fresh variety of today's market farmers and gardeners.

2 tablespoons olive oil or butter

2 medium yellow summer squash, peeled, halved, and thinly sliced

6 scallions, white part only, chopped (about ¾ cup)

2 cups snap peas or fresh lima or fava (broad) beans, precooked for 10 minutes in simmering water

3 ears corn, kernels removed with a sharp knife or 1½ cups corn kernels

½ teaspoon salt

½ teaspoon freshly ground black pepper

1 tablespoon chopped fresh mint

1 tablespoon chopped fresh parsley

1. Heat the oil in a large skillet over medium-high heat, add the squash and scallions, and sauté for 2 minutes. Cover the skillet and cook 5 minutes longer.

2. Add the snap peas, corn, salt, and pepper. Cover and heat through, about 2–3 minutes.

3. Sprinkle with mint and parsley. Serve immediately.

Yield: 8 servings

traditional succotash

Succotash was a Native American dish cooked in different forms (*sukquttahash*, *msak-watash*, *m'sick-quatash*) by various tribes throughout the North American continent. More often than not, it was a mixture containing corn and lima beans, the two most widely grown vegetables in the Native American world, and was sweetened with bear fat or maple syrup. To the Narraganset Indians of the Northeast, who introduced it to the European settlers in the 1620s, the word *succotash* meant "fragments," and their "hodgepodge" stew always included dried beans and corn, if nothing else, when food was scarce. During the plentiful months of growing vegetables, hunting, and fishing, a variety of the land's bounty was added to their catchall pot of succotash.

The tribes in the Southwest, who farm-raised sheep and hogs, added a variety of meat cuts to their succotash stew. Squash, peppers, and onions also made it into the pot. When the Virginia settlers started to raise hogs that they received from England, they were able to include plentiful chunks of fresh meat, salt pork, and bacon, which added extra nourishment, fat, and flavor to their own evolving hodgepodge versions of the original corn and bean succotash.

boiled corn on the cob

This is one of the most pleasurable ways to eat corn. All too often, however, the deliciously tender, crunchy ears are overcooked. Personal preferences aside, when corn is sweet and crisp enough to eat raw, it needs to be cooked for only a couple of minutes. Count on at least two ears per person.

This recipe is for boiling corn. You can also cook it in the microwave, and you won't lose any nutrients to the water. Place shucked corn in a glass dish, cover with plastic wrap, and microwave on HIGH for 40 seconds per ear. To steam corn, place ½ cup of water in a large kettle, add the shucked corn, and cover. Bring to a boil and cook for 3–5 minutes. Remove the corn and serve immediately.

4 quarts water

8 ears sweet corn

1. Use a pot big enough to hold 4 ears of corn without crowding; bring the water to a boil.

2. While you're waiting for the water to boil, shuck the corn and remove the silks.

3. Drop 4 ears of corn at a time into the boiling water; cook for 1½–2 minutes. Remove with tongs; serve immediately.

4. In the same boiling water, cook the second batch of corn while eating the first.

Yield: 4 servings

flavored butters for corn

Flavored butters make ordinary corn on the cob an epicurean delight. They are also delicious on broiled fish or with dinner muffins and breads.

herb

1 cup (2 sticks) butter, softened and mashed

1 clove of garlic, minced

2 tablespoons chopped fresh herbs (recommended combinations: parsley and tarragon chives and cilantro sweet basil and lemon thyme dill and celery leaves rosemary and chives sage and apple mint)

½ teaspoon salt

½ teaspoon freshly ground black pepper

citrus-jalapeño

1 cup (2 sticks) butter, softened and mashed

2 tablespoons grated lime or lemon zest (first wash fruit)

2 teaspoons lime or lemon juice

1–2 jalapeño chiles, seeded and chopped (wear gloves when handling chiles), or 1 teaspoon grated fresh ginger and 1 teaspoon crushed dried chiles

½ teaspoon salt

½ teaspoon freshly ground black pepper

In a small bowl, mash all ingredients together. Transfer the butter to a container, cover, and refrigerate until ready to use. Refrigerate or freeze leftover butter.

Yield: 16 tablespoons

grilled corn

Grilling makes an interesting change from boiling or steaming corn and simplifies things when you're serving a lot of people. For a variation, cut the shucked ears into 1½- to 2-inch sections, grill them in foil, and serve with cherry tomatoes threaded on skewers.

8 ears sweet corn

½ cup (1 stick) butter

1 or 2 cloves of garlic, crushed or finely minced

½ teaspoon coarsely ground black pepper

16 sprigs fresh thyme, sage, rosemary, or basil

1. Prepare grill for medium heat.

2. Husk the corn.

3. In a small bowl, mash together the butter, garlic, and pepper.

4. Lay 1 herb sprig on each of 8 pieces of aluminum foil. Spread one side of the ears with half of the butter mixture and place each ear butter side down on top of the herb.

5. Spread the remaining butter mixture on the corn and lay another herb sprig over the top. Close the foil.

6. Place the foil-wrapped ears on a grill rack 4 inches above the heat. Grill for 20–25 minutes, turning the corn every 4–5 minutes.

Yield: 4 servings

corn roasted on the grill

This is the way Native Americans cooked corn, though they put the unhusked ears directly into the hot ashes to roast or covered them with a layer of earth, then piled hot coals on top.

8 ears unhusked sweet corn

½ cup (1 stick) flavored butter (optional)

salt and freshly ground black pepper (optional)

1. Prepare grill for medium heat.

2. Because the ears are too hot to handle when they come off the grill, it's better to peel back the husks and remove the silks before roasting the corn. To do this, carefully peel the husks down to where they meet the stem and remove the silks. If desired, flavored butters, salt and pepper, or other seasonings can be added at this point. Fold the husks back around the ears and secure them with strips of foil.

3. Place the corn on top of a grill rack directly over medium heat. Cover the grill and roast the corn for 20 minutes, giving them quarter turns every 5 minutes.

4. Serve immediately with butter and salt and pepper, if desired. Or remove the corn from the cob and use the kernels in salsa or another dish.

Yield: 4 servings

pan-roasted kernels

Pan-roasting fresh kernels until they are golden brown brings out their nutty flavor, and it's faster than cooking whole ears on the grill. Start with a dry skillet over medium-high heat. Add the kernels and roast without stirring for 5 minutes. Stir and roast 5 minutes longer, until brown. If desired, add a drizzle of olive oil halfway through if the kernels are sticking, but don't add enough to "fry" the corn. Add salt and pepper to taste and serve atop fish, potatoes, salads, meats, grains, and soups.

stir-fried summer corn medley

Stir-frying means superfast cooking, and nothing stir-fries faster than fresh sweet corn. Combining the corn with tiny cherry tomatoes, sweet and hot peppers, and fresh-picked basil is nothing short of savoring a bite of summer. I stir-fry in a flat-bottomed, nonstick wok.

1 tablespoon olive oil

1 large orange, green, or purple bell pepper, halved horizontally and cut into thin strips

1 ripe purple or red jalapeño chile, seeds removed and cut into thin strips (wear gloves when handling chiles)

3 scallions, sliced

1 pint cherry or grape tomatoes

2 cloves of garlic, finely minced

4 ears corn, kernels removed (2 cups)

¼ cup shredded fresh sweet Italian basil leaves

½ teaspoon salt

½ teaspoon freshly ground black pepper

1. Place the wok over high heat and add the oil. When the oil is hot, stir-fry the bell pepper, jalapeño, and scallions for 2 minutes.

2. Add the tomatoes and garlic and cook 2 minutes longer.

3. Add the corn, basil, salt and black pepper and cook 1–2 minutes longer.

Yield: 6–8 servings

creamed corn

I'm not crazy about creamed vegetables, but creamed corn is something else. You can make this dish with heavy cream, whole milk, or low-fat milk.

2 tablespoons butter

2 tablespoons all-purpose or whole wheat flour

1–1¼ cups low-fat or whole milk or light cream or a combination

2 cups corn kernels, or 4 ears corn with kernels removed (if using canned corn, substitute the corn liquid for an equal quantity of the milk)

1 teaspoon curry powder (optional)

¼ teaspoon salt

¼ teaspoon freshly ground black pepper

1. Melt the butter in a 2-quart saucepan over a low heat.

2. Stir in the flour and cook for 1 minute.

3. Add the milk and stir or whisk until smooth and thick, about 3 minutes.

4. Add the corn, curry powder (if desired), salt, and pepper and cook gently for 2 minutes. Remove from the heat and serve immediately.

Yield: 4–6 servings (3 cups)

creamed corn II

Husk 4 ears of corn. Stand them in a bowl. Using a sharp knife, slice through the kernels to release the milk. Remove the kernels; scrape the remaining juices from the cob. Put two-thirds of the corn and all the milky juice in a food processor; purée until smooth. Melt 4 teaspoons of butter or heat 2 tablespoons of cream. Add the reserved kernels; cook, covered, on low for 2 minutes. Add the puréed corn, salt, and pepper. Cook over medium heat for 2 minutes. Add more cream, butter, or water, as needed. Top with fresh chives or parsley.

basic polenta

When serving polenta as a savory dish, I like to flavor it with 1 to 2 tablespoons of chopped fresh or dried herbs and 2 to 4 tablespoons of grated or crumbled cheese, such as blue, Cheddar, or reduced-fat herb spread. Serve piping hot from the pan topped with maple syrup (for breakfast) or tomato sauce (for dinner). Or spoon the hot polenta into a flat-bottomed dish sprayed with cooking oil. Allow the polenta to cool at room temperature or refrigerate it. When it is solid, cut it into squares and fry, grill, or bake them for a breakfast or dinner side dish.

6½ cups water

2 cups coarse cornmeal

1 teaspoon salt

1. In a large pot, bring the water to a rolling boil.

2. Reduce the heat and pour in the cornmeal in a thin, slow stream, stirring constantly and rapidly with a wooden spoon or a whisk.

3. Add the salt; continue stirring for about 5 minutes. Lower the heat and simmer for 20 minutes, stirring occasionally. The polenta is done when it comes away from the sides of the pan.

Yield: 6–8 servings

polenta primer

Living in Geneva, Switzerland, for seven years during the 1960s was my passport to sampling many European cuisines. Northern Italian food became my passion, and polenta, a ridiculously simple dish of cooked cornmeal, numbered among my favorite recipes.

Polenta is a dish for all seasons. In the United States, where it has become very popular in recent years, it is served most often as a starter topped with a mélange of wild and domestic mushrooms or melted Gorgonzola cheese. In Continental Europe, I have found it more often served as an accompaniment to chicken or game and covered with a rich, meaty brown gravy or a flavorful vegetable–tomato sauce. Some of my friends make it for breakfast and serve it piping hot topped with a knob of fresh local butter and mascarpone cheese, and sometimes drizzled with honey.

Traditionally, polenta is made from stone-ground or coarse yellow cornmeal that is cooked slowly for about 25 minutes on top of the stove. You can reduce the time by cooking it in the microwave or using instant polenta meal, which cooks in about 15 minutes. A speedier method still is to buy rolls of prepared polenta. Sold in the refrigeration section of the supermarket, premade polenta is ready for slicing and baking, broiling, or pan-frying. (Don't cook it in the microwave or you will end up with rubber.)

There are many ways to enjoy polenta. Whether served hot from the pan or chilled and sliced, then broiled or pan-fried with a little butter or olive oil, polenta is the perfect base for fried eggs and warm corn salsa; grated Cheddar cheese and sliced scallions; slivers of fresh mozzarella and tomato sauce; roasted red bell peppers and shaved Parmesan; curried chicken and corn; and anything else that tastes good on pasta, bread, or pastry. Leftover polenta can also be spooned into a bowl and chilled, ready to be turned into a savory side dish.

roasted corn for
relishes, garnishes,
salads, and soups

My favorite method of
roasting corn on the grill
is with the husks removed.
I like to eat roasted corn
out of hand, and I also use
this technique when I want
to add roasted corn to a
recipe. Simply husk the corn
and remove the silks. Roll
the ears in olive oil and
sprinkle them with pepper
and, if desired, ground
spices or dried herbs. You
can also roll the ears in
chopped fresh herbs or lime
juice. Place the ears on an
oiled rack on the grill about
4 inches above medium
heat. Cover and grill for
15 to 20 minutes, giving
quarter turns every 5 minutes, until the ears are
evenly grilled and lightly
charred.

corn, tomatoes, and zucchini

This is a good way to use summer's bountiful crops of tomatoes, zucchini, and corn — from your garden or the farmers'
market. I like to serve this dish over brown rice with broiled
halibut steaks, summer bluefish, or Spanish mackerel.

2 tablespoons olive or
vegetable oil

1 large red onion, sliced
paper thin

2 cloves of garlic, minced
or crushed

2 medium zucchini, washed
or peeled and thinly sliced

6 large, juicy-ripe tomatoes,
cut into ½-inch wedges

2 tablespoons fresh thyme
leaves or shredded fresh
cilantro

6 ears corn, kernels removed
(about 3 cups)

½ teaspoon salt

½ teaspoon freshly ground
black pepper

1. Heat 1 tablespoon of the
oil in a large skillet and sauté
the onion and garlic for 5 minutes over high heat. Add the
remaining oil to the skillet,
stir in the zucchini, and sauté
5 minutes longer.

2. Add the tomatoes and
thyme, reduce the heat to
medium low, and simmer for
15 minutes.

3. Increase the heat to medium
high, add the corn, cover, and
cook 3–5 minutes longer.
Remove from the heat, season
with the salt and pepper, and
serve immediately.

Yield: 8 servings

4

MAIN COURSES

I add corn to many of my recipes, not only because I love its sweet flavor but also because it provides a splash of color when combined with dark green vegetables or when tossed on top of salad or into soup or stew. In fact, you can toss 1 cup or so of whole kernels into practically any dish — meat, fish, or chicken — without diffusing the flavor or altering the liquid content. Not only will the addition of corn increase the nutritional quality of any dish but there will also be more servings to go around.

curried chicken and corn in patty shells

This simple dish takes next to no time to prepare, and it never fails to please. You can substitute leftover turkey or a can of red salmon for the chicken. I often make a white sauce and use puréed fresh, canned, or frozen corn kernels. Served with a green salad or al dente steamed broccoli, this dish is as pretty as it is tasty.

4 frozen patty shells

3 cups Creamed Corn (see recipe on page 111)

1 cooked whole chicken breast, cut into ½-inch cubes

2 teaspoons mild curry powder

1. Preheat the oven to 450°F. When it's hot, place the patty shells on a baking sheet, reduce the temperature to 425°F, and bake for 20 minutes.

2. While the shells are baking, combine the corn, chicken, and curry powder. Heat gently for 10 minutes, or until hot.

3. Remove the shells from the oven and scoop off the lids.

4. Spoon the corn and chicken mixture into and around the shells. Serve immediately.

Yield: 4 servings

chicken corn pie

When time is limited, make the cornbread topping for this recipe from a cornmeal biscuit or pancake mix. You may also decide to simmer the chicken on the stove, then top it with dumplings made from the cornmeal mix.

4 tablespoons olive or vegetable oil

1 large onion, thinly sliced

1 stalk of celery, thinly sliced

1 carrot, thinly sliced

3 cloves of garlic, minced

one 4-pound chicken, skinned and cut into serving pieces

3 tablespoons all-purpose flour

1½ cups low-sodium chicken broth or vegetable juice

1 tablespoon ground coriander

1 teaspoon ground cumin

½ teaspoon freshly ground black pepper

¼ teaspoon cayenne pepper

1 Regular Cornbread batter (see recipe on page 32)

1. Preheat the oven to 425°F.

2. Heat 1 tablespoon of the oil in a large skillet; add the onion, celery, carrot, and garlic and sauté over low heat for 3 minutes. Remove to a dish.

3. Roll half of the chicken pieces in half of the flour and heat 1½ tablespoons of the remaining oil. Sauté the chicken over medium heat, turning to brown each side, about 4 minutes. Remove and add the chicken to the reserved vegetables.

4. Repeat step 3 with the remaining chicken, flour, and oil.

5. Return the sautéed chicken and vegetables to the skillet; add the broth, coriander, cumin, black pepper, and cayenne.

6. Cook over medium heat, stirring until the sauce thickens, about 2 minutes.

7. Pour the mixture into a deep 2½- to 3-quart baking dish and top with the batter.

8. Bake for 25 minutes.

Yield: 4–6 servings

chicken enchiladas

For a change of pace, you may want to use this as a stuffing or topping for corn-meal pancakes, waffles, polenta, corn tortillas, cornbread, or savory biscuits (see Index on pages 184–87 for those recipes). Serve this dish with a variety of easy side dishes, such as crushed kidney beans heated with ½ cup of sliced scallions, yellow rice (add 1 teaspoon of ground turmeric to the water), sliced avocado, and shredded romaine lettuce.

cooking oil spray

1 pound boneless chicken breast

¼ cup water

6 tablespoons cream cheese

2 tablespoons chunky salsa, mild or hot

1 tablespoon olive or vegetable oil

1 small onion, chopped

3 cloves of garlic, crushed

1 can (28 ounces) crushed tomatoes

1 can (3½ ounces) green chiles, chopped (wear gloves when handling chiles)

1 tablespoon ground coriander

eight 6-inch tortillas

1½ cups sour cream

¼ cup chopped fresh chives or scallion greens

1. Preheat the oven to 400°F. Spray a 9- by 12- by 2-inch baking dish with cooking oil.

2. Put the chicken breasts into a skillet, add the water, cover, and simmer for 10 minutes.

3. Reserve the poaching liquid. Thinly slice the chicken.

4. Blend the reserved liquid, cream cheese, and salsa. Stir in the chicken.

5. Heat the olive oil in a large skillet and sauté the onion and garlic for 2 minutes.

6. Add the tomatoes, chiles, and coriander. Simmer for 15 minutes.

7. Warm the tortillas in the microwave or the oven (see box at right).

8. Spoon 2–3 tablespoons of the chicken mixture along the center of each warm tortilla. Roll them up and place them seam side down in the prepared baking dish.

9. Spoon the tomato sauce over the top; bake for 15 minutes.

10. Mix the sour cream and chives and spoon a little over each cooked tortilla.

Yield: 4–6 servings

how to warm tortillas

To make soft tortillas pliable, wrap them in wax paper or microwavable plastic wrap and microwave on HIGH until they are warm and flexible. Microwave 2 tortillas for 20 seconds, 3 or more for 40–50 seconds. Or wrap them in foil and warm them in a preheated 350°F oven for 10 minutes, until pliable.

Alternatively, fold each tortilla in half. Spray a large nonstick skillet with cooking oil, if desired, or heat the tortillas — one or two at a time — in a dry skillet over low heat for approximately 1 minute on each side.

ginger-basted roast chicken with whole corn stuffing

Nothing could be simpler than roasting a chicken, especially if you make stuffing as a side dish. If you decide to stuff the chicken, don't pack it into the cavity — leave it loose so that heat can penetrate the interior, then bake the rest separately. Add 5 minutes extra per pound to the cooking time for a stuffed chicken.

one 6-pound roasting chicken

1½ cups Ginger Basting Sauce (see recipe on facing page)

1 teaspoon ground ginger

½ teaspoon salt

½ teaspoon freshly ground black pepper

2 cups Whole Corn Stuffing (see page 96)

1 cup applesauce

1. Preheat the oven to 450°F. Place the chicken in a large roasting pan and loosen the skin on the breast to form pockets.

2. Spoon 1 tablespoon of the basting sauce into each pocket. Pour 2 tablespoons of the sauce over the entire chicken and put 1 tablespoon into the cavity.

3. Sprinkle the ginger, salt, and pepper over the chicken. If you are cooking all of the stuffing inside the chicken, spoon it into the cavity at this point. (Or spoon it all into a baking dish and place in the oven for the last 30–40 minutes of roasting time. See Stuffing on page 97.)

I do not truss the chicken (tie the legs together).

4. Place the chicken in the oven and roast for 15 minutes. Reduce the heat to 400°F and baste the chicken with ¼ cup of the sauce. Loosely tent the chicken with aluminum foil.

5. Roast the chicken 45 minutes longer (75 minutes if it is stuffed), basting with the sauce three or four more times. Remove the foil and cook 15 minutes longer.

6. To see whether the chicken is done, slit the skin inside the thigh next to the rib cage. If the flesh is too pink, make a longer slit in the skin to slightly expose the uncooked meat. Do the same on the other thigh. Baste the chicken with any remaining sauce or the pan juices and roast 10–15 minutes longer, if necessary.

7. When the chicken is done, transfer it to a serving platter. To make gravy, pour the pan juices into a small saucepan (skim off the fat or use a fat separator), warm over medium heat, and stir in the applesauce, adding more to taste.

Yield: 4–6 servings

ginger basting sauce

1 cup apple juice

¼ cup marsala, light sherry, or red wine

¼ cup olive oil

2 scallions, thinly sliced

1 tablespoon freshly grated ginger

Combine all ingredients in a screw-top jar and shake vigorously.

Yield: 1½ cups

crock-pot chicken thighs

This dish is so easy and so good, and the best thing about it is that when you sit down to eat, you have the wonderful feeling of having done nothing. I don't thicken the juices, because I serve it over baked potatoes or rice. If you like thick gravy, blend 2 tablespoons of cornstarch in 1 tablespoon of water and stir the mixture into the hot liquid 5 minutes before you're ready to serve.

3 stalks of celery, thinly sliced

1 green bell pepper, diced

1 medium onion, thinly sliced

8 chicken thighs, skin and fat removed

6 cloves of garlic, crushed

1 teaspoon dried thyme

½ teaspoon ground allspice

½ teaspoon salt

½ teaspoon freshly ground black pepper

1 cup apple or carrot juice or low-sodium chicken broth

1 cup tomato or vegetable juice

2 cups corn kernels

1. Turn a Crock-Pot to HIGH.

2. Place the celery, bell pepper, and onion on the bottom of the pot and put the chicken on top.

3. Sprinkle with the garlic, thyme, allspice, salt, and black pepper.

4. Pour the apple and tomato juices over the top.

5. Cover and cook for 4 hours on HIGH (Crock-Pots vary, so refer to your owner's manual). Add the corn and cook 1 hour longer.

Yield: 4 servings

tomatillo and chorizo on cheese grits

Spicy sausages are a taste-tingling foil for the blandness of grits. Spanish chorizo is available in many markets, including those in areas with large Hispanic populations. You can also use andouille or spicy Italian sausage. This spicy mixture makes a delicious topping for baked grits or polenta (see recipe on page 112). When making Grits and Cheese Pudding (see recipe on page 28), stir it into the cornmeal preparation at the same time you add the cheese.

8 ounces spicy chorizo or Italian sausage, casings removed

1 medium red bell pepper, chopped

1 small or medium onion, chopped

2 cloves of garlic, minced

2½ cups fresh or canned tomatillos, puréed

⅓ cup fresh cilantro leaves, or 2 tablespoons fresh oregano leaves, chopped

¼ teaspoon salt

¼ teaspoon freshly ground black pepper

8 servings grits (see recipe page 27), or Grits and Cheese Pudding (see recipe page 28)

1. Crumble the chorizo into a large skillet and cook for 5 minutes over medium heat.

2. Add the bell pepper, onion, and garlic and cook 10 minutes longer.

3. Add the tomatillos, cilantro, salt, and black pepper and cook over low heat 15 minutes longer.

4. Place a serving of grits on each of 8 plates and top with the sausage mixture.

Yield: 8 servings

argentine puchero

This is similar to what is called "hot pot" in the British Isles, and a very delicious stew it is. You can stretch this recipe by adding 4 yellow potatoes (cut in rough chunks) when you return the chicken and lamb to the pot.

2–3 tablespoons olive oil

3½–4 pounds chicken, skin removed, meat cut into chunks

1 pound lean, boneless lamb, cut into 2-inch cubes

4 medium onions, thinly sliced

1 large carrot, sliced

5 cloves of garlic, crushed

two 8-inch yellow squash, or ½ small peeled pumpkin, cut into ½-inch cubes

1 tablespoon dried thyme

⅛ teaspoon cayenne pepper

4 cups tomatoes, chopped

2 cups fat-free, salt-reduced chicken broth

1 cup red wine

3 cups corn kernels

3 tablespoons cornstarch

2 tablespoons water

1. Heat 1 tablespoon of the oil in a 5- to 6-quart Dutch oven and sauté the chicken for 2 minutes on each side. Remove to a plate.

2. Add the lamb to the pot and brown on all sides for a total of 2 minutes. Remove to a plate.

3. Heat 1 more tablespoon of the oil in the pot and sauté the onions, carrot, and garlic for 5 minutes.

4. Add the remaining oil, if necessary, along with the squash, thyme, and cayenne and sauté 3 minutes longer.

5. Return the chicken and lamb to the pot; cover with the tomatoes, broth, and wine. Simmer for 45 minutes.

6. Add the corn and simmer 10 minutes longer.

7. Combine the cornstarch and water to make a smooth paste and stir it into the hot liquid; cook for 5 minutes to thicken the stew.

Yield: 6–8 servings

ethnic stews

Whether you know them as hot pot, hotchpot, hotchpotch, *hutspot*, or hodgepodge, the message is clear. These ethnic stews are a hodgepodge, which is Middle English for a mixture, jumble, gallimaufry, mishmash, hash, or potpourri. They were created to make use of a region's bounty, which in most cases was plenty of mutton (the meat from "lamb" older than 12 months), potatoes, and onions. Classic hotchpots are assembled in layers — first lamb is browned, then vegetables topped with potatoes are added, then the ingredients are covered with broth and baked or simmered on top of the stove. I have dined on a variety of these mutton hotchpotches in widely disparate places, including a classic Irish Stew at the renowned Ballymaloe House in County Cork, Ireland, a *blanquette d'agneau* in a farmhouse in the south of France, and a North of England Lancashire hot pot at my mother's table. According to the dictionary's definition of hotchpotch, even shepherd's pie and succotash, with their mixtures of chopped mutton and vegetables, can be classified as types of hodgepodge.

steak with grilled corn salsa

Try to marinate the flank steak for several hours, so that it absorbs the flavors. When fresh corn is no longer available, roast frozen corn kernels in a dry skillet (see page 109) over medium-high heat. It is not necessary to thaw the frozen kernels — they thaw fast in the hot skillet. Serve with rice or noodles and mixed greens.

1½ pounds flank steak or boneless sirloin steak

2 cups Marinating Sauce (see recipe on facing page)

4 cups Grilled Corn Salsa (see recipe on facing page)

1. Place the steak in a rectangular dish and cover it with ⅓–½ cup of the marinade. Marinate for 1–8 hours or overnight.

2. Prepare grill for medium-high heat.

3. Remove the steak from the marinade and place it on a grill rack directly over medium-high heat. Grill for 4–5 minutes on each side for rare or 7 minutes on each side for medium rare. Baste with ½ cup of the remaining marinade at the beginning and when turning the steak (discard any marinade that has touched the raw or cooking meat).

4. Remove the steak from the grill. Slice the meat across the grain into thin strips and arrange on a serving plate.

5. Drizzle with ½ cup of the remaining marinade (shake or stir it first) and top with a few spoonfuls of the salsa. Pass the remaining ½ cup of marinade and salsa at the table.

Yield: 4–6 servings

marinating sauce

1 cup olive oil

½ cup orange juice

¼ cup fresh lime juice

3–4 tablespoons jalapeño or herb-flavored mustard

6–8 cloves of garlic, minced

1–2 tablespoons fresh herb mixture of rosemary, thyme, and tarragon or freshly grated lime zest

½ teaspoon freshly ground black pepper

Combine all ingredients in a screw-top jar and shake vigorously to combine.

Yield: 2 cups

grilled corn salsa

2 tablespoons lime juice

2 tablespoons olive oil

3 ears corn, husked

4 medium ripe tomatoes, chopped

1 medium yellow or orange bell pepper, diced

2 scallions, thinly sliced

¼ cup chopped fresh cilantro leaves

2 cloves of garlic, minced

1 small fresh jalapeño chile, seeded and minced (wear gloves when handling chiles)

1. Prepare grill for medium heat.

2. Combine the lime juice and oil in a rectangular dish and roll the ears of corn in the mixture. Reserve the remaining liquid.

3. Place the corn on a rack directly over medium heat. Cover and grill the ears for 20 minutes, turning them two or three times.

4. Pour the remaining liquid into a medium bowl and add the tomatoes, bell pepper, scallions, cilantro, garlic, and jalapeño. Toss to combine.

5. Remove the grilled kernels from the cobs with a sharp knife and add them to the tomato mixture.

Yield: 4 cups

ham and cheese tortilla strata

This recipe goes together so fast that it's perfect for brunch with weekend guests (big ones or little ones). However, you may also want to serve it for dinner and substitute cooked chicken, turkey, or veggie-soy crumbles for the ham. If desired, salsa and sour cream can be served on the side.

cooking oil spray

3 cups Tomato Salsa (see page 25)

twelve 6- or 8-inch corn tortillas

1½ cups chopped cooked ham

2 cups grated cheese (Cheddar, Monterey Jack, or a mixture)

½ cup sliced jalapeño chiles (wear gloves when handling chiles)

½ cup sliced scallions

1. Preheat the oven to 350°F. Lightly spray a 15- by 11-inch baking dish with cooking oil.

2. Spread 1 cup of the salsa in the bottom of the dish and arrange 4 of the tortillas on top.

3. Layer 1 more cup of the salsa on top and sprinkle with ¾ cup of the ham and ⅔ cup of the cheese.

4. Layer 4 more of the tortillas, the remaining salsa, the remaining ham, and ⅔ cup of the cheese.

5. Top with the remaining tortillas and cheese.

6. Cover with foil and bake for 15 minutes. Remove the foil and bake 10–15 minutes longer.

7. Remove from the oven and sprinkle with the jalapeños and scallions.

Yield: 6 servings

mexican strata

Serve with chopped jalapeño chiles, sour cream, and yellow rice. (Add ½–1 teaspoon of ground turmeric to the water in which the rice is cooked.)

cooking oil spray

9 flat corn tostadas

1½ cups corn kernels

1½ cups canned kidney beans, rinsed and drained

1½ cups grated plain or jalapeño Monterey Jack cheese

1 small green bell pepper, finely chopped

1 small onion, chopped

2 cups crushed tomatoes

2 cloves of garlic, crushed

½ teaspoon chili powder

½ teaspoon ground cumin

1. Preheat the oven to 350°F and spray a 2-quart soufflé or casserole dish with cooking oil.

2. Break the tostadas in half and arrange 6 of the pieces on the bottom of the dish.

3. Layer ½ cup each of the corn, beans, and cheese over the tostadas. Sprinkle with one-third of the pepper and onion. Repeat with the remaining tostadas, corn, beans, cheese, pepper, and onion to create two more layers.

4. Combine the tomatoes, garlic, chili powder, and cumin. Pour over the top layer.

5. Bake for 40 minutes.

Yield: 6 servings

shepherd's pie

This variation of an old favorite replaces the usual minced lamb or beef with soy protein. When I include it in vegetarian cooking classes, it never fails to gain converts. If you prefer, substitute ground turkey or beef for the veggie ground round.

1½ tablespoons olive or vegetable oil

2 medium carrots, thinly sliced

2 medium stalks of celery, thinly sliced

2 medium onions, chopped, or white part of 1 large leek, thinly sliced

4–6 cloves of garlic, crushed

2 small zucchini, washed and sliced (optional)

8 ounces cremini mushrooms, sliced

2½ cups carrot or vegetable juice, or ½ cup red wine

¼ cup chopped parsley

1 tablespoon chopped fresh sage or thyme leaves or both, or 1½ tablespoons dried mixed herbs

¼–½ teaspoon salt

¼–½ teaspoon freshly ground black pepper

12 ounces veggie ground round or extra-firm tofu, cut into ½-inch cubes

2 cups corn kernels, fresh, frozen, or canned and drained

4 medium yellow potatoes, boiled and mashed with ¼ cup fat-free milk

2 tablespoons grated cheese (optional)

1. Preheat the oven to 375°F.

2. Heat 1 tablespoon of the oil in a 12- to 13-inch skillet over medium heat.

3. Sauté the carrots, celery, onions, and garlic for 3 minutes.

4. Drizzle the remaining oil into the skillet, add the zucchini, if desired, and mushrooms, and sauté 2 minutes longer.

5. Add the carrot juice, parsley, herbs, salt, and pepper, then stir in the veggie ground round and the corn.

6. Heat for 3–5 minutes. Spoon the mixture into a 2½-quart casserole, and top with the potatoes.

7. Bake for 20 minutes. Sprinkle the cheese, if desired, over the potatoes.

Yield: 4–6 servings

tamales with vegetarian fillings

Invented by the Aztec Indians, tamales — both sweet and savory — are wildly popular today. You can find them on the menus of Latin American restaurants and at specialty tamale restaurants that feature as many as 30 different fillings. Serve with rice, guacamole, extra bean filling, salsa, and sour cream on the side.

16–20 packaged corn husks (see box on page 133) or 4 ears fresh corn

3 cups Masa Dough (see recipe on page 132)

2½ cups filling (see recipes on pages 132–33)

1. If using husks from fresh corn, carefully remove them from the ears a day ahead of time so they can dry. Ideally, you want to work with husks that are at least 6 inches wide and 8 inches long. Leave the kernels on the cobs, enclose everything in an airtight plastic bag, and refrigerate.

2. Before using the packaged or the fresh husks, soak them in warm water for 30 minutes, until pliable. Remove from the water just before filling them and pat dry with paper towels. Place them with the tips facing away from you.

3. Spoon 3 tablespoons of dough onto 12 of the husks and use a spatula to spread it into a 5- by 6-inch (or thereabouts) rectangle on each husck, leaving a margin around the husk of 1 inch at both the top and the bottom and ½ inch down each side.

4. Spoon 2½ tablespoons of the filling down the middle of the dough and fold the right side of the husk over to the center of the filling. Fold the left side slightly over the right side to seal the packet. Fold the bottom and top to meet in the center. Cut the remaining husks into strips and use them to tie each end of the tamale closed.

5. When all the tamales have been assembled, place them seam side down on a rack in a large steamer and add water to just below the rack. Cover and bring the water to a boil over high heat. Reduce the heat to low and steam the tamales for 45 minutes. Allow them to rest for 3 minutes before serving.

6. Place two tamales on each plate and serve hot.

Yield: 6 servings

masa dough

2 cups *masa harina* flour

2 teaspoons baking powder (optional for a lighter dough)

½ teaspoon salt

1–1¼ cups water

¾ cup soft shortening (authentic recipes use lard)

1. In a medium-sized bowl, mix the flour, baking powder (if desired), salt, and water.

2. Beat in the shortening.

3. Cover the bowl with plastic wrap to prevent the dough from drying out.

Yield: 3 cups, enough for 12 tamales

corn and cheese filling

Although this recipe is a good choice for a lacto-vegetarian dinner, the fresh corn mixture can be replaced with 3 cups of cooked spicy ground beef.

1 large banana pepper (those used for chile rellenos)

1 small onion

2 cups corn kernels, fresh or frozen

½ cup grated Monterey Jack cheese

½ cup chunky taco sauce, mild, medium, or hot

1. In a food processor, quickly blend the banana pepper and the onion.

2. Add the corn and process for about 10 seconds.

3. Add the cheese and taco sauce and pulse just to blend.

Yield: 2½ cups, enough for 12 tamales

bean chipotle filling

Pork and beef are traditional tamale fillings. But you can fill tamales with anything that would be suitable in crêpes, wontons, and egg rolls, such as shrimps, cheese, beans, potatoes, vegetables, or meat loaf. For sweet fillings, try fresh or dried fruits, preserves, chopped nuts, and shredded coconut. You can use these fillings in tortillas and burritos as well.

1 tablespoon olive or vegetable oil

1 small onion, finely chopped

2 cloves of garlic, crushed

1 cup canned black beans, rinsed and drained

1 cup canned pinto beans, rinsed and drained

2 chipotle peppers in adobo sauce, chopped

½ cup shredded fresh cilantro

½ teaspoon ground cumin

1. Heat the oil in a large skillet over medium heat, add the onion and garlic, and sauté for 5 minutes.

2. Add the black beans and pinto beans and cook 2 minutes longer. Crush the mixture with the back of a spoon.

3. Add the peppers along with 1 tablespoon of the sauce, the cilantro, and cumin. The filling should be firm; if it seems too stiff, add 1 tablespoon of warm water or more adobo sauce.

Yield: 2½ cups, enough for 12 tamales

corn husks for tamales

Although you can use the husks from fresh corn, you may find it easier to buy packets of husks. Purchased husks are easier to work with because they are all the same size. Four ears of fresh corn will provide 16 to 20 workable husks — more than the number of tamales you are making but sufficient to allow for any tearing during assembly or for overlapping two small ones. Fresh or packaged, husks must be soaked in warm water before you can use them. You can find packaged husks (as well as *masa harina* flour, another important tamale ingredient) at Hispanic markets, or order them from catalogs and online sources (see Resources, pages 181–183).

soy: the other kind of protein

During the past decade, there has been an explosion of products processed from soybeans. It's now possible to find a wide variety of tempeh and textured soy-protein burgers, sausages, ground round, ham, and chicken. Tempeh can be grilled, stir-fried, or stewed and eaten in both hot and cold dishes. Tofu, made from the curds of soymilk, is produced in several textures: soft, medium, firm, and extra firm. The "silken" type of tofu, whether soft or extra firm, is shelf-stable but breaks down very easily. Tofu blocks are packed in water; they must be kept under refrigeration but can also be frozen.

The dish you are making will determine the texture of tofu you should use. Choose silken, soft, and medium tofu for puréeing into creamy dips, sauces, soups, and shakes and to replace eggs or cream in pie fillings and custards. The refrigerated blocks of firm and extra-firm tofu (some brands come smoked or seasoned) are best for slicing, dicing, and cubing for use in stir-frys, casseroles, kabobs, and broiled or grilled dishes. Medium and firm tofu are good for crumbling and scrambling with chopped vegetables and for combining with herbs and grated vegetables or mashed beans for molding into patties. Scrambled tofu mixtures and fried tofu patties can be stuffed into pita pockets, taco shells, soft tortillas, or crêpes.

Because plain tofu is so mild, you may want to marinate it before using it. To give it a meatier texture, drain off the marinade and sauté the pieces in a nonstick skillet for 3 to 5 minutes on each side. For a crispy outer texture, fry tofu in a little oil over high heat for 2 minutes on each side. Freezing will also give tofu a chewier, more meatlike texture. For ideas on how to use tofu, see the recipes on pages 60, 76, 90, and 130.

polenta gnocchi

As an alternative to frying, you can arrange the gnocchi in a greased dish, cover with tomato vegetable sauce, and bake at 350°F for 20 minutes.

4 cups water

1 cup cornmeal

1 egg, beaten

¼ cup grated Parmesan cheese

6 tablespoons olive oil

½ teaspoon coarsely ground black pepper

3 cups Tomato Salsa (see recipe on page 25)

1. Bring the water to a rolling boil and stir in the cornmeal in a slow, steady stream. Continue stirring for 5 minutes.

2. Simmer, stirring frequently, 15 minutes longer.

3. Remove from the heat and beat in the egg, cheese, 2 tablespoons of the oil, and pepper.

4. Spoon the mixture into a flat-bottomed rectangular or square dish and smooth it down until it is about 1 inch thick. Refrigerate for 2 hours.

5. Preheat the oven to 125°F.

6. Slice the polenta gnocchi into 1-inch pieces.

7. Heat 2 tablespoons of the remaining oil in a large, heavy skillet until medium hot and cook half of the gnocchi, turning once after 2 minutes. Fry until golden brown. Remove to a plate lined with paper towels and place in the oven to keep warm. Repeat with the remaining oil and gnocchi.

8. Place the gnocchi in a serving dish and top with warm tomato salsa.

Yield: 4–6 servings

sweet corn risotto

When Michael Kramer, executive chef of McCrady's Restaurant in Charleston, South Carolina, shared this recipe with me, he said it was his customers' favorite risotto, probably because the corn adds such a sweet quality. His favorite sweet corn is the old-fashioned Silver Queen, which he folds in with the tomato at the end so that it adds to the fresh color of the finished dish. Chef Kramer serves this risotto as an entrée with salad or as a side dish with grilled chicken. He also uses the scraped cobs to flavor the broth — just one of the ways in which he uses the entire ear of corn.

2 ears fresh corn

3 cups chicken broth

2 cups water

¼ cup olive oil

¼ cup finely chopped onion

2 teaspoons minced garlic

2 cups (14 ounces) Arborio rice

⅔ cup dry white wine

4 tablespoons (½ stick) unsalted butter, cut into pieces

1 cup finely grated Asiago cheese (about 6 ounces)

1 small tomato, finely chopped

¼ cup finely chopped fresh chives

salt

1. Working in a shallow bowl, remove the corn kernels from the cobs, then scrape each cob with a knife to extract the juice. Reserve the cobs.

2. Bring the broth, water, and cobs to a simmer over medium heat. Continue to simmer the mixture while you go on to the next steps.

3. Heat the oil in a 3-quart saucepan over medium heat and sauté the onion for 5 minutes, until soft. Add the garlic and sauté 30 seconds longer.

4. Add the rice and sauté, stirring constantly, 1 minute longer. Add the wine and simmer, stirring constantly, until all of the liquid is absorbed.

5. Add 1 cup of the simmering broth and cook the rice at a strong simmer, stirring constantly, until the broth is absorbed.

6. Continue simmering and adding broth, about ½ cup at a time, stirring constantly and letting each addition become absorbed before you add the next, until the rice is creamy but al dente, about 18 minutes total. (You probably will use only about 2½ cups of the broth. For softer rice, continue stirring and adding more liquid.)

7. Remove the pan from the heat and stir in the butter and ½ cup of the cheese.

8. Gently fold in the corn kernels and their juice, the tomato, and the chives and stir until the butter and cheese have melted, then season to taste with salt. Thin the risotto with leftover broth, if desired, and serve sprinkled with the remaining ½ cup of cheese.

Yield: 4 servings

She stood breast high amid the corn,
Clasp'd by the golden light of morn,
Like the sweetheart of the sun,
Who many a glowing kiss had won.
—THOMAS HOOD (1799–1845), *Ruth*

corn soufflé

To make this into an eye-pleasing lunch or dinner, sprinkle the soufflé with paprika and serve with fresh tomato sauce or pesto.

cooking oil spray

1 cup low-fat milk

½ cup cottage cheese

½ cup finely grated Parmesan cheese

3 tablespoons all-purpose flour

2 tablespoons olive or vegetable oil

¼ teaspoon freshly ground black pepper

⅛ teaspoon ground nutmeg or mace

3 egg yolks

1½ cups corn kernels (if using canned corn, substitute ¼ cup of the liquid for ¼ cup of the milk)

4 egg whites

1. Preheat the oven to 375°F and spray a 1½-quart, 3-inch-deep soufflé dish or other pan with cooking oil.

2. Blend together the milk, cottage cheese, Parmesan, flour, oil, pepper, and nutmeg.

3. Pour the mixture into a saucepan and heat gently for 4 minutes, stirring frequently.

4. Remove the mixture from the heat and stir in the egg yolks. Add the corn.

5. In a large bowl, beat the egg whites until stiff. Pour one-third of the milk mixture into the whites and blend.

6. Gently fold in the rest of the milk mixture just until a lumpy batter is formed.

7. Pour the mixture into the prepared soufflé dish and cut a circle in the top with a knife about 1 inch from the edges.

8. Bake for 30 minutes. Serve immediately.

Yield: 4 servings

cornmeal cheese soufflé

Serve this soufflé with any of the relishes or tomato sauces in the other chapters.
Or use a prepared chunky chipotle, poblano, black bean, or tomato salsa.

cooking oil spray

2 cups low-fat milk

½ cup cornmeal or quick-cooking (not instant) grits

3 tablespoons butter

¾ cup grated jalapeño or plain Jack cheese

½ teaspoon ground cumin

¼ teaspoon freshly ground black pepper

3 eggs, separated

1. Preheat the oven to 350°F and spray a 1½-quart soufflé dish or straight-sided casserole dish with cooking oil.

2. In a double boiler, heat the milk until it is almost boiling.

3. Add the cornmeal and the butter. Cook for 10 minutes, stirring occasionally, until the mixture becomes a thick batter.

4. Remove from the heat; beat in the cheese, cumin, pepper, and egg yolks.

5. In a large bowl, beat the egg whites until stiff. Fold the cornmeal mixture into the whites and pour the batter into the prepared dish.

6. Bake for 35–40 minutes, until puffed and golden brown. Serve immediately.

Yield: 4 servings

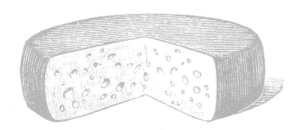

corn quiche

I love quiches and consider them all-purpose dishes — I am happy to eat them for breakfast or lunch, as an appetizer, or as the main dish for dinner. Make them with or without a crust. If you prefer quiche with a crust but don't want the bother of making your own pastry, pick up a commercial crust from the freezer section of your supermarket. Or fit (overlapping and trimming slightly, where necessary) two or three flour or corn tortillas into the bottom of the pie plate and you'll have a fine, fast crust base for your quiche.

cooking oil spray

1 tablespoon olive or vegetable oil

1 small onion, or 4 shallots, chopped

1½ cups low-fat milk

1 cup cottage cheese

3 eggs

1½ cups corn kernels (if using canned or frozen corn, drain thoroughly)

½ cup grated Cheddar cheese

¼ teaspoon ground mace

¼ teaspoon ground nutmeg

¼ teaspoon freshly ground black pepper

pastry for one 9- or 10-inch quiche (see recipe on facing page)

1 egg white, beaten

1. Preheat the oven to 425°F. Lightly spray with cooking oil a 9- or 10-inch quiche dish (or use a 2-inch-deep pie plate).

2. Heat the oil in a skillet and sauté the onion for 2 minutes. Place in a large bowl.

3. Add the milk, cottage cheese, and eggs and beat together.

4. Stir in the corn, Cheddar, mace, nutmeg, and pepper.

5. Roll out the pastry to about ⅛-inch thickness. Fit it into the pie plate, trim it ½ inch above the rim, and flute the edges. Brush the bottom and sides with the egg white.

6. Pour the filling into the pastry and bake for 10 minutes. Reduce the heat to 350°F and bake 30 minutes longer, until a knife inserted into the center comes out clean.

7. Let cool for about 10 minutes before cutting into wedges.

Yield: 4–6 servings

pastry

1 cup all-purpose flour

⅓ cup whole wheat flour

½ cup (1 stick) cold butter

2–3 tablespoons ice-cold water

1. Combine the all-purpose and whole wheat flours in a large bowl.

2. Cut the butter into small pieces. Using a pastry blender or two knives, combine with the flour until the mixture resembles peas.

3. Add the water, 1 tablespoon at a time, until a ball forms.

4. Place the dough on a sheet of wax paper, press into a circle, cover, and refrigerate.

Yield: pastry for one 9- or 10-inch quiche

sweet potato and corn hash with grilled portobello mushrooms

The combination of sweet potato and corn produces such a flavorful and colorful dish. Yellow or white potatoes make a delicious alternative to the sweet potatoes. To serve, spoon the corn hash on top of the grilled mushrooms.

2 sweet potatoes, or 4 yellow or white potatoes, scrubbed

cooking oil spray

1½ cups corn kernels, fresh or frozen

2 scallions, thinly sliced

2–3 tablespoons olive oil

½ teaspoon salt

½ teaspoon freshly ground black pepper

4 large (about 6 inch) portobello mushrooms, caps wiped and stems discarded

4 tablespoons homemade or prepared basil pesto

2 tablespoons red wine or balsamic vinegar

1. Place the potatoes in a glass dish, cover with plastic wrap, and microwave on HIGH for 5 minutes. Or boil or steam them for 10–15 minutes. Cool.

2. Spray a large skillet with cooking oil, add the corn, and sauté over medium-high heat for 3 minutes, until the kernels begin to brown. Add the scallions; sauté 2 minutes longer.

3. Remove the skins from the sweet potatoes. Cut into 1-inch cubes. Add to the skillet along with 1 tablespoon of the olive oil and the salt and pepper.

4. Sauté 20 minutes longer; add more oil halfway through and reduce the heat to medium low. Remove to a bowl.

5. Spray the skillet with cooking oil. Add the mushrooms (skin side down), spoon about 1 tablespoon of the pesto into each, and drizzle the remaining olive oil around them. Cover and cook over medium heat for 5 minutes.

6. Remove the cover, add the wine, and cook 5–10 minutes longer, reducing the heat to medium low, if necessary.

7. Place the mushrooms on individual plates and top each with a spoonful of potato hash. Arrange more hash around each mushroom.

Yield: 4 servings

macaroni, cheese, and corn casserole

Comfort food is always welcome in any home, and this is one of my family's favorites.

cooking oil spray

8 ounces elbow macaroni or twists, cooked al dente as the package directs (4 cups cooked)

2 tablespoons butter

2 tablespoons all-purpose flour

2 cups low-fat milk

1¼ cups grated Cheddar cheese

½ teaspoon freshly ground black pepper

¼ teaspoon ground nutmeg

1½ cups corn kernels

¼ cup grated Parmesan cheese

2 tablespoons fresh bread-crumbs

1. Preheat the oven to 350°F and lightly spray with cooking oil a 2-quart ovenproof casserole dish.

2. Melt the butter in a saucepan and stir in the flour. Cook for 1 minute.

3. Add the milk and whisk until the sauce is smooth. (If using canned corn, substitute the liquid for some of the milk.)

4. Remove from the heat and stir in the Cheddar, pepper, and nutmeg.

5. Add the macaroni and corn to the sauce. Pour into the prepared casserole dish.

6. Sprinkle the top with the Parmesan and breadcrumbs and bake for 25 minutes.

Yield: 4 servings

corn products

Cornmeal, or ground corn, which has been a staple food in some cultures for thousands of years, evolved out of necessity. The early types of corn grown by Native Americans produced kernels encased in a tough skin. To render the corn edible, people ground it between stones. To make this an easier task, native peoples first dissolved the hard hulls by soaking them in wood ashes and water, or they briefly boiled, dried, and roasted the kernels. In the Southwest, Native Americans ground the corn between slabs of soft sandstone, which left a residue in the meal and caused their teeth to wear down. The settlers also used grinding stones, but in the form of huge wheels powered by hand, water, and wind. Steel rollers replaced the mills' stone wheels during the 1850s. However, some mills still produce stone-ground cornmeal. Stone-ground corn is not only tastier but also more nutritious than steel-rolled corn (stone-ground corn contains the whole kernel, whereas steel rollers eliminate the oily corn germ, which is made into corn oil).

All cornmeal is nutritious (like oatmeal, it is second to wheat in protein content), and it is a boon to people who are allergic to the protein in wheat gluten. When cornmeal is used without the addition of wheat or gluten flour, the results are dense and coarse. However, a lighter product can be obtained by replacing one-third to one-half of the cornmeal with all-purpose, rye, or whole-wheat flour (though the last two won't provide quite the same leavening action as the first). Using baking powder and/or baking soda also creates a rising action in baked goods and, if still more volume is desired, well-beaten egg whites will increase the air content.

Cornstarch (known as corn flour in Europe) is obtained from the endosperm layer of the kernel and is used commercially in baked goods, canned gravies, and baking powder. It is also used to make laundry starch.

Corn syrup, which is made from cornstarch, is used in the confectionery trade to give a smoother texture to frostings, chocolate, and desserts. In particular, light corn syrup is used to produce clear jams and jellies and the syrup for canned fruits. In fact, few food products on supermarket shelves do not contain corn syrup. It's in breads, cakes, cookies, cereals, and many other products.

Masa dough is a moist dough made of ground nixtamal (dried corn soaked in lime water and then cooked). *Masa harina* is a corn flour made from cooked and dehydrated masa. Sometimes called instant masa or tamale or tortilla flour, masa harina is more commonly available from than fresh masa, which doesn't have a long shelf life. Masa harina can be rehydrated into fresh masa dough by adding water and sometimes lard or oil.

To derive a number of corn by-products, processors separate the kernel into four components: starch, germ oil, fiber, and protein. The starch, for example, is converted into dextrose, which is fermented to produce ethanol (for lead-free automotive fuels) and carbon dioxide (used in hydroponic greenhouses, carbonated beverages, and refrigeration equipment). The germ oil goes into cooking oils, margarine, mayonnaise, salad dressings, shortening, and soap. The hulls (fiber) and protein produce gluten feed and gluten meal; soluble portions are also used in foodstuffs.

huitlacoche quesadillas

Christy Velie, the chef at Café Atlántico (see page 62), inherited the idea for this dish from her Spanish colleague José Andrés. Whether it's enclosed in quesadillas or crêpes, *huitlacoche* (pronounced wheet-lah-koh-shay) stuffing is a favorite with the lunchtime crowd. See Resources on page 181–183 for mail-order suppliers.

2 tablespoons olive oil

1 small jalapeño chile, finely diced (wear gloves when handling chiles)

1 teaspoon minced garlic

1 pound *huitlacoche*, frozen or canned

2 cups fresh corn kernels

2 cups Basic Sofrito (see recipe at right)

1 bunch fresh cilantro, stems discarded, leaves chopped

3 sprigs fresh epazote or coriander, stems discarded, leaves chopped

½ teaspoon salt

eight 10-inch tortillas

1. Preheat the oven to 400°F.

2. Heat the oil in a large pan over medium heat and sauté the jalapeño and garlic for 3 minutes.

3. Add the *huitlacoche*; cook until all water has evaporated.

4. Add the corn and sofrito and bring to a boil. Remove from the heat.

5. Add the cilantro, epazote, and salt.

6. Stuff each tortilla with ½ cup of the mixture, fold in the ends, roll up the sides, and place on a lightly oiled baking sheet; bake for 15 minutes, until crisp.

Yield: 8 servings

basic sofrito

1 tablespoon olive oil

1 cup chopped onion

3 cloves of garlic, minced

2 cups chopped fresh or canned tomatoes, with juice

1. Heat the oil in a skillet over medium heat. Add the onion and garlic; sauté for 5 minutes.

2. Add the tomatoes; cook over low heat for 30–45 minutes.

Yield: 2 cups

huitlacoche

Mexican and Latin American chefs covet *huitlacoche* (also called *cuitlacoche*) for its rich, earthy taste in much the same way other chefs treasure black or white truffles. An edible fungus that grows on corn, it was discovered by the Aztecs, who named it *huitlacoche*, or "black excrement." Modern-day epicureans translate it into more appealing names, such as maize mushrooms and Mexican truffles. American corn growers call it corn smut and burn the mushroom-shaped fungal balls before they can burst and release thousands of black spores. However, like their neighbors in Mexico, some specialty farmers in the United States are coming to regard *huitlacoche* as a marketable delicacy and grow plots of corn inoculated with the fungus spores. When the mushroomlike growths develop, they are cut off the corn at an early, silver-gray stage and sold fresh. They are also sold frozen and canned. *Huitlacoche* balls are sliced and sautéed with garlic and other seasonings, then stuffed into quesadillas, omelettes, crêpes, and tacos or added to sauces and soups. Some chefs add it to ice creams and desserts as well.

smoked salmon quesadillas

Quesadillas are baked or toasted in a skillet. I make them into sandwiches, layer and stack them, and fold them over omelette style. I fill them with leftovers or create special fillings. For the most part, I consider them light fare, something I can whip together in 5 minutes. Smoked salmon is a fitting filling for lunch, brunch, or appetizers; for a more satisfying dinner combination, use sliced turkey or chicken or grilled tuna or flank steak. Traditional quesadillas contain cheese.

four 8- or 10-inch flour or corn tortillas

½ cup Corn and Chickpea Hummus (see recipe on page 86)

2 scallions, thinly sliced

8 ounces smoked salmon, sliced

freshly ground black pepper

garlic-flavored cooking oil spray (optional)

1. Spread each tortilla with 2 tablespoons of the hummus, sprinkle with scallions, add 3–4 slices of salmon, and grind black pepper to taste on top.

2. Fold each tortilla in half. Spray a large nonstick skillet with cooking oil, if desired, or toast the quesadillas — one or two at a time — in a dry skillet over high heat for approximately 2 minutes on each side.

3. Serve whole or cut into two or three wedges.

Yield: 4 servings

fish posole

In the Southwest, posole is a stew made with hominy. The Aztecs called dried hominy *nixtamal*, and the method of preparing and boiling the kernels to soften them was called *posole*. Try substituting chicken or pork (and add 1 teaspoon of chili powder, if desired) for the fish and increase the cooking time by 30 minutes. Make a vegetarian version by doubling the onion and adding 1 cup each of chopped bell pepper and summer or winter squash. Serve with guacamole and soft, warm tortillas (see box, "How to Warm Tortillas," on page 119).

1 tablespoon olive oil

1 red onion, finely chopped

4 cloves of garlic, crushed

8 cups vegetable or low-salt chicken broth or water

2 cans (16 ounces each) whole yellow or white hominy, rinsed and drained, if desired

1 can (3½ ounces) green chili peppers (mild or hot), chopped

½ teaspoon ground cumin

¼–½ teaspoon dried hot chili pepper flakes

1½ pounds monkfish or cod fillet, cut into 2-inch pieces

1½ pounds medium shrimps, shelled and deveined

1. Heat the oil in a 6-quart Dutch oven and sauté the onion and garlic for 5 minutes.

2. Add the broth, hominy, chili peppers, cumin, and chili pepper flakes.

3. Bring to a boil, reduce the heat, and simmer partially covered for 10 minutes.

4. Add the fish and shrimps and simmer 5 minutes longer.

5. Remove from the heat and serve immediately.

Yield: 6–8 servings

chilean sea bass primavera

With its red, green, and yellow colors, this is a very festive dish. If you prefer, you can replace the sea bass with mahi mahi, monkfish, deep-sea scallops, shrimps, or chicken breast cut into 1-inch chunks. I sometimes vary the flavor by using 1 teaspoon of chopped fresh ginger root and fresh basil leaves in place of the tarragon. I like to serve this with brown or jasmine rice and Curry Mayonnaise.

2 tablespoons olive or vegetable oil

2 medium red bell peppers, thinly sliced

3 cloves of garlic, minced

2 pounds Chilean sea bass, cut into 2-inch pieces

1 tablespoon fresh tarragon

½ teaspoon salt

½ teaspoon freshly ground black pepper

2 cups corn kernels, fresh or frozen

2 cups young sugar snap peas, no more than 2 inches long

2 tablespoons chopped chives or scallion greens

1 cup Curry Mayonnaise (see recipe on facing page)

1. Heat the oil in a large skillet over medium heat, add the bell peppers and garlic, and sauté for 2 minutes.

2. Add the sea bass, tarragon, salt, and pepper. Cook, stirring, for 5 minutes. (If substituting scallops or shrimps, cook for 1 minute only.)

3. Add the corn and peas, cover the skillet, and cook 5 minutes longer. (Cook only 2–3 minutes if using scallops or shrimps.)

4. Arrange on plates and sprinkle with the chives.

Yield: 4 servings

curry
mayonnaise

1 cup homemade or prepared mayonnaise

2 cloves of garlic, crushed (optional)

1 tablespoon honey

1 tablespoon lime juice

1 teaspoon curry powder

¼ teaspoon ground ginger

In a small bowl, thoroughly combine all ingredients. Cover; refrigerate until ready to use.

Yield: 1 cup

healthfulness of fish

Seafood offers the same high-quality protein as red meat — it has all the essential amino acids needed to build and repair body tissue. However, seafood contains less total fat, and it is low in saturated and high in polyunsaturated fatty acids. Research studies show that seafood's omega-3 fatty acids — especially those contained in fattier fishes, such as salmon, rainbow trout, shad, bluefish, mackerel, and (to a lesser extent) tuna — are effective in lowering cholesterol and triglycerides in the blood.

lime-marinated grilled salmon with corn salsa

Simplicity at its best, this recipe, adapted from *The Santa Fe School of Cooking Cookbook*, was shared by Susan Curtis, author of the book and owner of the school (see the profile on page 103). This entrée kicked off the first of the school's Contemporary Southwest Cooking classes, and it's still one of their favorites.

2½ cups Lime Marinade (see recipe on facing page)

2 pounds salmon fillets, cut into 4- to 5-ounce portions

salt freshly ground black pepper

2½ cups Corn, Tomato, and Black Bean Salsa (see recipe on facing page)

1. Pour half of the marinade into a glass baking dish, place the salmon on top, and cover with the remaining marinade.

2. Marinate for at least 1 hour at room temperature or refrigerate overnight.

3. Prepare grill for medium heat.

4. Remove the salmon from the marinade, wipe dry, and sprinkle with salt and pepper to taste. Grill over medium heat to desired doneness, about 4–5 minutes on each side.

5. Place the salmon fillets on a large platter or individual plates and top each serving with a spoonful of salsa. Serve extra salsa on the side.

Yield: 6–8 servings

lime marinade

2 cups coarsely chopped onion

⅓ cup fresh lime juice

1 tablespoon honey

1 bunch fresh cilantro, stems discarded and leaves coarsely chopped

2 large jalapeño chiles, minced (wear gloves when handling chiles)

1½ teaspoons coarsely chopped garlic

1 teaspoon salt

Combine all ingredients in the bowl of a food processor and pulse for 30 seconds. Cover and refrigerate until ready to use.

Yield: 2½ cups

corn, tomato, and black bean salsa

2 tablespoons olive oil

½ cup finely chopped onion

1 teaspoon minced garlic

3 tablespoons coarsely chopped fresh cilantro

2 tablespoons cider vinegar

1 tablespoon Red Chile Honey (see Resources on pages 181–183)

1 jalapeño chile, minced (wear gloves when handling chiles)

1 teaspoon salt

¼ teaspoon freshly ground cumin seed, lightly toasted

3 large ripe Roma (plum) tomatoes, chopped

1 cup cooked black beans

¾ cup fresh corn kernels

1. Heat the oil in a skillet over medium heat, add the onion and garlic, and sauté for 5 minutes, until soft. Remove from the heat.

2. In a medium-sized bowl, combine the cilantro, vinegar, honey, chiles, salt, and cumin.

3. Add the onion mixture, tomatoes, beans, and corn and let the mixture sit for 30–45 minutes to allow the flavors to blend.

Yield: 2½ cups

blue corn tortilla–encrusted fish

This recipe can be made with any lean white fish, so use the kind your family likes best. Some brands of tortilla chips can be crushed very easily, while others are a little tougher. A good way to crush them is to place them between sheets of wax paper or in a brown paper bag and go over them with a rolling pin. Serve this dish with mashed or roasted potatoes or potato salad and salsa or relish.

cooking oil spray

⅓ cup sour cream or processed egg product, or 1 egg, beaten

1 tablespoon lemon juice

½ teaspoon ground cumin, chili powder, curry powder, or paprika

½ teaspoon salt

½ teaspoon freshly ground black pepper

1½ cups finely crushed blue corn (or other) tortilla chips

1½ pounds flounder, tilapia, skinned red snapper, or other lean fish fillets

1. Preheat the oven to 450°F. Spray a baking sheet or a 13- by 9- by 2-inch baking dish with cooking oil. (If desired, first line the baking sheet or dish with aluminum foil.)

2. Combine the sour cream, lemon juice, cumin, salt, and pepper in a shallow dish. Place the chips on a large plate.

3. Cut large fish fillets into serving pieces. Dip each piece into the sour cream mixture and then into the chips, to coat both sides. Arrange the fillets on the baking sheet.

4. Bake, uncovered, for 10–12 minutes, until the fish flakes when tested with a fork.

Yield: 4 servings

deep-sea scallop sauté

If you prefer, substitute monkfish cut into 2-inch chunks for the scallops. This dish is good over pasta twists or jasmine rice.

2 tablespoons olive oil

one 6-inch zucchini, julienned into 1- by ¼-inch-thick strips

1 red bell pepper, cut into ½-inch pieces

3 cloves of garlic, crushed or minced

6 whole scallions, sliced

1½ teaspoons grated lime or lemon zest

½ teaspoon salt

½ teaspoon freshly ground black pepper

1½ cups tomato sauce

¼ cup cream

1 pound deep-sea scallops, sliced in half horizontally

1½ cups corn kernels

¼ cup chopped fresh parsley

1. Heat the oil in a large skillet over medium heat and sauté the zucchini, bell pepper, and garlic for 3 minutes.

2. Add the scallions, zest, salt, and black pepper and sauté 2 minutes longer.

3. Add the tomato sauce and cream and cook for 2 minutes, until the mixture is hot.

4. Add the scallops and corn, lower the heat, and simmer for 5 minutes, or until the scallops are cooked through.

5. Remove to a large serving bowl and sprinkle with the parsley.

Yield: 4 servings

shrimps with tomato, corn, and basil sauce on a bed of linguine

This fast and easy dish is excellent with rice as well. Although I make this recipe more frequently with fresh "frozen" shrimps purchased at the market, I always try to keep one pound of frozen, shelled (not cooked) shrimps on hand for last-minute meals. You can also substitute extra-firm tofu for the shrimps.

1 tablespoon sesame oil

3 cloves of regular garlic, crushed

1 clove of elephant garlic, thinly sliced

2 cups corn kernels, fresh (4 ears of corn), frozen, or canned and drained

3 ripe tomatoes, diced, or 1¼ cups stewed tomatoes, cut into chunks

½ tablespoon freshly ground black pepper

¾ pound fresh or frozen shrimps, shelled, or 8 ounces extra-firm tofu, cut into 1-inch cubes

1 handful fresh Thai Queen of Siam, cinnamon, or Italian basil leaves, shredded

8 ounces linguine, cooked al dente as the package directs

1. Heat the oil in a large skillet over medium heat. Add the crushed garlic and sauté for 30 seconds. Add the sliced elephant garlic and sauté 30 seconds longer.

2. Add the corn, tomatoes, and pepper and cook for 3 minutes.

3. Add the shrimps and cook over medium heat for 3 minutes, until they are no longer opaque and are beginning to turn a uniform pale pink. (If using tofu, heat for 3–4 minutes longer to allow the tofu to absorb more of the flavors.)

4. Add the basil and turn off the heat.

5. Spoon the mixture over the pasta and serve immediately.

Yield: 2 servings

5

SNACKS & SWEETS

corn's natural sugar makes it a perfect addition to healthful snacks and sweets. People are once again adopting the Colonial practice of using every part of the ear. Fresh, juicy kernels are milked or puréed and used to thicken and sweeten sauces and puddings. Even the corncobs are used to infuse ice cream with flavor. And, of course, popcorn, an American favorite, is a perfect base for a wide range of flavors and ingredients.

popcorn snack mix

Kids will enjoy having this (healthful) snack in their lunch boxes or when they arrive home from school.

4 cups popped corn (¼ cup unpopped)

1 cup alphabet cereal

1 cup corn cereal squares

1 cup cinnamon graham squares

½ cup raisins

½ cup sunflower seeds

In a large bowl, thoroughly combine all ingredients. Transfer the mixture to an air-tight plastic container to store.

Yield: 8 cups, 6 servings

nutty honey popcorn

For variety, try different nuts or sweeteners.

8 cups popped corn (½ cup unpopped)

1 cup roasted peanuts or almonds

¼ cup butter or butter-flavored oil

¼ cup honey, molasses, or maple syrup

1 teaspoon ground cinnamon

1. Preheat the oven to 250°F.

2. Place the hot popped corn in a large roasting pan and add the nuts. Mix well.

3. Melt the butter in a skillet over low heat; add the honey and cinnamon.

4. Stir the butter mixture into the popcorn and nuts and bake for 15 minutes.

5. Cool and serve.

Yield: 4 servings

peanut butter popcorn

Try variations on this recipe. You can use dried cranberries, cherries, or other fruit instead of raisins, or replace peanut butter with tahini (but use less of it).

8 cups popped corn (½ cup unpopped)

2 cups raisins

½ cup chunky peanut butter

¼ cup honey or molasses

1. Place the hot popped corn in a large serving bowl, add the raisins, and mix well.

2. In a skillet over low heat, melt the peanut butter and molasses until you can blend them together.

3. Pour the peanut butter mixture over the popcorn and raisins and toss to combine.

Yield: 6 servings

great country farms, bluemont, virginia

When brothers Bruce and Mark Zurschmeide bought acreage in Bluemont, Virginia, in 1992, their intention was to join the Community Supported Agricultural Scheme (CSAS), which allows people to buy shares in the annual crop production of local farms. In return for an annual fee, members receive a weekly supply of freshly picked fruits and vegetables. Operated by Mark's wife, Kate, the farm's market is also a local and regional favorite for its bounty of fresh produce, pick-your-own strawberries, and free-range eggs.

The Zurschmeides grow several varieties of bicolor, white, and yellow sweet corns. "Every year we try different varieties," says Bruce, the corn man of Great Country Farms. In 2001, when he grew a new variety called Seneca Airhead, he says, "We got immediate calls from our members saying, 'This is the best corn we've ever had.' We need to grow good-tasting corn that holds up after picking," he continues, "because when we deliver it to members' houses, it may sit there for a few hours. It's important to pick corn early in the morning, when it's at its coolest temperature, and then get it into a cooler quickly."

Bruce also grows several popping corn varieties, including strawberry corn, yellow finger corn, and multicolored Indian corn. "Popping corn," he says, "has to be real dry, and the best way to dry it is to hang it for four to six weeks." Their special "kettle" popping corn is in great demand at local parties. Mixed with sugar and oil, the kernels are dropped into hot stainless-steel kettles heated with propane gas. When the kernels pop, they are quickly removed to a copper kettle and seasoned with salt.

skillet popped corn

For the best and most authentic popped corn, Bruce Zurschmeide of Great Country Farms (see profile on facing page) recommends using the old-fashioned method of popping corn in a skillet on top of the stove. For extra flavor, he adds 1 teaspoon of garlic powder as soon as the kernels begin to pop but waits until all the popping has stopped before adding salt to taste. (If you are using an electric popper or microwave popcorn, follow the manufacturer's directions.)

2 tablespoons safflower oil

½ cup popcorn kernels

1. Warm a large, deep, heavy skillet over medium-high heat.

2. Add the oil so that it just covers the bottom of the skillet.

3. After 1–2 minutes, add a few kernels; when one pops, pour in the rest.

4. Stir the kernels until they are all coated with oil.

5. Cover the skillet with a vented lid (to let steam escape) and shake the popping kernels to make sure they are evenly heated. Continue shaking the skillet until the popping slows down; remove from the heat.

Yield: 8 cups

the history of popcorn

You may think of popcorn as a favorite movie snack, but it has been in vogue for several thousand years — not smothered in butter but coated in the ashes from Native American fires. Native Americans used it for food, necklaces, decoration, and currency. Magical powers were attributed to popcorn. It was strewn about doorways as a sign of hospitality and to ward off enemies. It was also a symbol of fertility. The person who first dropped a kernel at the edge of a fire and witnessed the hard seed exploding into fluffy white softness must have thought it magic, indeed. When popcorn kernels are heated, the moisture contained in the starchy center of each kernel turns to steam, which expands and pushes against the hard shell until it bursts open and turns inside out. To early indigenous peoples without grinding tools, this phenomenon turned the hard-hulled seeds into an important food source.

The early settlers learned about popcorn when Quadequina, an Algonquin Indian, contributed a deerskin bag of popped strawberry corn to the Thanksgiving feast. The Pilgrims learned how to "parch" their own corn and served it with milk as a breakfast cereal. They also made Indian *nookick* — popped and pulverized corn — by popping corn in earthenware pots placed on hot ashes or in a metal perforated cylinder set next to the fire and turned by an axle. And some 1,500 years ago, indigenous peoples popped corn in huge clay or metal pots (sometimes with tripod legs) set over a fire — not so very different from the modern-day method of making kettle corn (see Great Country Farm Profile on page 160).

Toward the end of the 19th century, popcorn left the hearthside and was peddled on the streets and at carnivals. Charles Cretors turned it into the fad that it is today. He invented the popcorn "machine" and developed the method of popping corn in oil. Around the same time, R. W. Rueckheim began selling a sticky mixture of popcorn and peanuts coated with chewy molasses. He called his confection Cracker Jack, a brand name that is still around today. In 1945, Percy Spenser discovered that corn kernels could be popped under microwave energy. When microwave ovens became mainstream household fixtures in the early 1980s, the popcorn industry exploded. Today, Americans consume 17.5 billion quarts of popcorn a year.

exotic popcorn

While most varieties expand to 20 to 30 times their kernel size, some "gourmet" popcorns expand 40 times. Dried sweet corn also expands a little when heated, and this corn is usually referred to as parched or puffed corn.

Popcorn comes in white, yellow, black, red, blue, and multicolored varieties. Supermarkets sell white and yellow kernels; colored and gourmet popcorns are available at specialty food stores, through mail-order catalogs, and on the Internet. Williams-Sonoma sells gourmet red, white, and yellow popping corns, as well as old-fashioned hand-turned poppers. You can buy red and blue popcorns from the Santa Fe School of Cooking Market. The multicolored Indian corn sold at farmers' markets in the fall can also be used for popping.

Basically the same complex carbohydrate food that Native Americans ate thousands of years ago, popcorn is a healthful, high-fiber, low-fat, low-calorie snack. One cup of plain popcorn contains only 25 calories (50 with butter or oil). Eating popcorn doused in butter and salt satisfies our basic taste cravings for fat and salt. However, you can enjoy big flavors by using low-fat seasonings, such as Italian mixed herbs and Mexican and Asian spices.

shoepeg and basil pesto bites

Shoepeg corn is an old-fashioned sweet variety that is no longer popular for eating fresh because the kernels are small and thin and have somewhat tough skins. They resemble pine nuts in appearance and sweetness and are ideal for stirring into pesto. Refrigerate any leftover pesto in a tightly sealed container (plastic or glass) and it will stay fresh for several weeks. Use the leftovers as a dip for toasted tortillas, bread, or crackers; as a topping for pasta, rice, and vegetables; or in stir-fries and soups.

2 packed cups fresh basil leaves

½ cup olive oil

¼ cup chopped walnuts

2 cloves of garlic

¼ teaspoon salt

1 can (11 ounces) shoepeg corn, drained

4 corn muffins or toaster corn muffins split in two, 8 squares of cornbread, 2 quartered corn tortillas, or 8 refrigerated and baked canned cornbread dough spirals

cooking oil spray

1. Preheat the oven to 425°F.

2. Place the basil, oil, walnuts, garlic, and salt in a food processor and purée.

3. Remove to a bowl and stir in the corn.

4. Place one generous teaspoon of pesto atop each muffin half.

5. Lightly spray a baking sheet with cooking oil, arrange the muffin halves on it, and bake for 10–12 minutes. (You can also make these in a toaster oven.) Remove and serve warm or at room temperature.

Yield: 8 servings, 2½ cups of pesto

cottage cheese and corn dip

Use this low-fat dip for crackers, stuff it into pita, or spread it on toasted English muffins. Stir in some herbs, curry powder, or Szechuan or Thai (peanut) sauce.

1 cup low-fat small-curd cottage cheese

½ cup cooked or canned corn kernels, drained

¼ cup shredded fresh basil, cilantro, or parsley, or 2 teaspoons dried mixed herbs

¼ cup thinly sliced scallions

½ teaspoon freshly ground black pepper

Combine the ingredients in a small bowl. Use immediately or cover tightly and refrigerate for up to 3 days.

Yield: 1½ cups

pita pizzas

If preferred, substitute English muffins split in two. Or combine the toppings, stuff into pita pockets, wrap in foil, and bake as mini calzones.

cooking oil spray

four 6-inch pitas, split

½–¾ cup spaghetti sauce

½–¾ cup corn kernels

1 teaspoon dried oregano

½ cup shredded low-fat mozzarella cheese

1. Preheat a toaster oven or a conventional oven to 425°F.

2. Lightly spray a baking sheet with cooking oil and place the pita halves on it. Spread with the sauce, then sprinkle with the corn, oregano, and cheese.

3. Bake for 10–15 minutes, until the cheese melts.

Yield: 4 servings

blue cornmeal shortcakes and berries

These shortcakes will be a hit whether you use blue, white, or yellow cornmeal.

1¼ cups presifted all-purpose flour

¾ cup blue cornmeal

4 tablespoons sugar

1 tablespoon baking powder

2 tablespoons butter

¾ cup milk

2 cups strawberries

2 cups blueberries

1 tablespoon corn syrup

1. Preheat the oven to 450°F.

2. Combine the flour, cornmeal, 2 tablespoons of the sugar, and baking powder in a medium-sized mixing bowl.

3. Cut in the butter with a pastry blender or two knives until the mixture resembles crumbs.

4. Stir in the milk.

5. Put the dough on a floured board and knead it for 1 minute. Pat it to a ½-inch thickness; cut it into 2-inch circles with a biscuit cutter or a small glass.

6. Place the dough on an ungreased baking sheet and bake in the middle of the oven for 10 minutes.

7. Slice the strawberries and sprinkle them with the remaining sugar. In a separate bowl, mash the blueberries with a fork and add the corn syrup; mix well.

8. Remove the shortcakes from the oven. Split them in half, spoon the strawberries on each bottom half, and cover them with the shortcake top. Pass the blueberry sauce at the table. Serve warm.

Yield: 8 to 10 servings

blue corn

The kernels of blue corn are deep blue with a purple cast. When ground, they produce a gray-blue cornmeal, which takes on a lavender shade when mixed with liquid. Blue cornmeal can be substituted for yellow and white cornmeal in most recipes.

The Navajo and Hopi Indians of the southwestern states have grown blue, black, and red corn for centuries. They prefer the blue corn for grinding into cornmeal for their daily needs. Native Americans believe that blue corn provides strength, and sick people often eat blue cornmeal mush *(atole)* or soup two or three times a day. Others prefer to dilute blue cornmeal with water and drink it.

The traditional Hopi bread, *piki,* is made from blue cornmeal, sage ashes (to preserve the blue color), and water. The mixture is boiled into a thick paste, which is kneaded and then thinned with more water until it reaches the consistency of dropping batter. A smoothly polished flat stone is greased with fat from the brain or spinal cord of a sheep or goat and heated over a wood fire until it is hot enough to sizzle a drop of water. The batter is then spread thinly over the stone by hand. When cooked, the papery bread is peeled off and rolled into *piki.*

Although tortilla factories are the major processors of blue corn, smaller producers also supply specialty food stores with blue cornmeal, pancake mixes, and whole dried kernels. See Resources, pages 181–183, for mail-order addresses.

blueberry and sweet corn slump

Slumps are similar to cobblers and are made with any fruit or fruit combination. The new sweet corns are so much like candy that they add natural sweetness to fruit desserts. One of my favorite combinations is corn and blueberries. This recipe doesn't call for a thickening agent, so there is a lot of juice. If you prefer a thicker sauce, substitute creamed corn for the whole kernels or add 2 tablespoons of flour to the granulated sugar.

1 cup cornmeal

1 cup all-purpose flour

½ cup brown sugar

1 tablespoon baking powder

5 tablespoons plus 1 teaspoon (⅓ cup) butter

½ cup low-fat milk

1 teaspoon vanilla extract (optional)

3 cups blueberries

2 cups sweet corn kernels, fresh or frozen

⅓ cup granulated sugar

1. Preheat the oven to 400°F and butter a deep 2-quart baking dish.

2. Combine the cornmeal, flour, brown sugar, and baking powder in a large bowl.

3. Cut in the butter with a pastry blender or two knives until the mixture resembles coarse breadcrumbs.

4. Stir in the milk and vanilla, if desired, until the dry ingredients are just moistened.

5. Mix the blueberries and corn in the baking dish; sprinkle with the granulated sugar.

6. Drop the batter on top of the blueberry-corn mixture.

7. Bake for 35 minutes.

Yield: 6 servings

orange cornbread pudding

As a child in England, I enjoyed many steamed and baked puddings made from flour or bread and containing ingredients that varied with the seasons or the contents of the pantry. They were studded with dried fruits, fresh apples, rhubarb, berries, or stem ginger or flavored with marmalade, golden syrup, treacle, or chocolate. Here is a variation on a childhood favorite.

4 cups diced cornbread (half of the Regular Cornbread recipe on page 32)

juice (½ cup) and grated zest of 1 medium orange (wash the skin before zesting and zest before juicing)

3 eggs

¼ cup granulated sugar

1½ cups low-fat milk

¼ cup orange marmalade, or 3 tablespoons brown sugar

1. Preheat the oven to 350°F. Butter a 2-quart baking dish.

2. Place the cornbread in a large mixing bowl and cover it with the orange juice.

3. Beat the eggs with the zest and granulated sugar.

4. Heat the milk and marmalade in a small saucepan. When bubbles form around the edges, slowly pour it into the egg mixture, stirring constantly, until it thickens sufficiently to coat the back of a spoon.

5. Pour the hot custard over the cornbread and stir gently to combine.

6. Spoon the batter into the prepared baking dish and set in a large pan. Pour boiling water into the pan until it reaches halfway up the sides of the dish.

7. Carefully place the pan in the oven and bake for 45 minutes, or until golden.

Yield: 6–8 servings

indian pudding

There are many versions of this famous Colonial dish. Some cooks go heavy on the molasses and butter; depending on your taste, you can double the quantities of the ingredients. For a richer pudding, use whole milk instead of low-fat. Serve warm with ice cream, if desired.

3 cups low-fat milk

⅓ cup molasses

¼ cup yellow cornmeal

¼ cup brown sugar

½ teaspoon ground cinnamon

½ teaspoon ground ginger

½ teaspoon ground nutmeg

3 eggs

2 tablespoons butter

ice cream or frozen yogurt (optional)

1. Preheat the oven to 300°F. Butter a 1½-quart baking dish.

2. Heat 2 cups of the milk and the molasses in a saucepan over low heat until bubbles form around the edges.

3. Add the cornmeal, a little at a time, stirring constantly. Cook for 10–15 minutes, stirring occasionally, until the mixture is thick. Remove from the heat.

4. In a small bowl, beat together the brown sugar, cinnamon, ginger, nutmeg, eggs, and remaining milk. Stir into the hot cornmeal mixture with the butter and beat until everything is thoroughly blended and the butter has melted.

5. Spoon the batter into the prepared baking dish and bake for 1½ hours.

Yield: 6 servings

variation: indian pudding with apples

In step 4, after beating in the butter, add 1 cup of peeled, cored, and diced tart apple (such as Granny Smith) to the batter. Spoon into the baking dish and bake as directed.

sweet corn and rice pudding with rum and lime sauce

This pudding may transport you back to the nursery for a minute or two, but it can be quickly turned into adult fare when drizzled with Rum and Lime Sauce.

butter-flavored cooking oil spray

1 cup corn kernels

1 cup cooked white rice (jasmine is particularly delicious)

3½ cups low-fat milk

6 egg yolks

½ cup sugar

¼ teaspoon ground cinnamon

¼ teaspoon ground nutmeg

⅔ cup Rum and Lime Sauce (see recipe at right)

1. Preheat the oven to 375°F. Spray six 6-ounce custard cups with cooking oil.

2. Mix the corn and rice; place ¼ cup of the mixture in each custard cup.

3. Combine the milk, egg yolks, sugar, cinnamon, and nutmeg. Pour the mixture into the cups to within ¼ inch of the top.

4. Place the cups in a large baking pan and pour boiling water into the pan until it reaches halfway up the sides of the cups.

5. Carefully put the pan in the oven and bake for 45–60 minutes, until the custard is firm.

6. Remove from the oven and chill for several hours.

7. To serve, unmold the puddings by turning each cup upside down onto an individual plate. Drizzle with the Rum and Lime Sauce.

Yield: 6 servings

rum and lime sauce

2 tablespoons butter

2 tablespoons dark brown sugar

⅓ cup dark rum

2 tablespoons fresh lime juice

1. Melt the butter in a skillet over medium heat.

2. Add the sugar, stir until melted, then add the rum and lime juice.

3. Simmer on low heat for 3–5 minutes.

Yield: ⅔ cup

cinnamon cornmeal cookies

These cookies have a crunchy but cakelike texture. Although I have added cinnamon, you may want to substitute your favorite flavor, such as ginger, grated lemon zest, or vanilla. Serve the cookies alone as a snack or with ice cream as a dessert.

corn beverages

Settlers and Colonial farming families often made "moonshine" out of corn; they also made corn juice, corn cider, corn beer, corn wine, and corn whiskey. Simple corn whiskey stills were commonplace in the 18th and 19th centuries.

1½ cups presifted all-purpose flour

½ cup cornmeal

1 teaspoon baking powder

1 teaspoon ground cinnamon

½ teaspoon baking soda

¾ cup brown sugar

½ cup (1 stick) butter

1 egg

½ cup buttermilk

½ cup finely chopped walnuts

cooking oil spray

1. Preheat the oven to 350°F.

2. Combine the flour, cornmeal, baking powder, cinnamon, and baking soda in a medium-sized bowl. Set aside.

3. In a large bowl, beat the brown sugar and butter until fluffy.

4. Add the egg and beat until combined. Stir in the buttermilk, then the walnuts. Add the flour mixture and blend well.

5. Use a teaspoon to drop the cookie dough 2 inches apart onto a baking sheet lightly sprayed with cooking oil. Bake for 10–12 minutes, remove from the oven, and place on a wire rack to cool.

Yield: About 48 cookies

ross edwards' blue heaven carrot cake

I'm happy to pass along this recipe for blue cornmeal carrot cake, which Ross kindly shared with me (see his recipe for Blue Blazes Hush Puppies on page 87). Ross doubles the recipe to make two loaf cakes. If you do the same, you may want to enclose one cake in a plastic freezer bag and freeze it for up to three months.

¾ cup (1½ sticks) butter, melted

½ cup plus 2 tablespoons honey

1½ teaspoons vanilla extract

2 eggs

1 cup all-purpose flour

1 cup blue cornmeal pancake mix (see Resources, pages 181–183)

1 teaspoon baking powder

1 teaspoon ground cinnamon

½ teaspoon ground allspice

¼ teaspoon baking soda

1¼ cups shredded carrots

1 tablespoon lemon juice

½ cup chopped walnuts or golden raisins

1. Preheat the oven to 350°F. Butter a 9- by 4-inch loaf pan.

2. In a large bowl, beat together the butter, honey, and vanilla. Beat in the eggs one at a time.

3. Sift together the flour, pancake mix, baking powder, cinnamon, allspice, and baking soda and stir about ½ cup at a time into the butter mixture. Alternate adding the flour mixture and the carrots until all ingredients have been incorporated and well blended.

4. Add the lemon juice and nuts.

5. Spoon the batter into the loaf pan and bake for 40 minutes, until a toothpick inserted into the center comes out clean. Remove the pan to a wire rack and cool for 10 minutes before turning out onto a plate.

Yield: 10–12 servings

cornmeal pear scones with caramel pecan sauce

The creation of Megan Moore of Moore Fine Food, a catering and fine foods store in Great Barrington, Massachusetts, these pear scones were served at a benefit dinner attended by Storey Publishing editor Dianne Cutillo. Swept off her feet, Dianne asked for the recipe and passed it along for inclusion in this book. I'm sure you'll agree that Megan has come up with a winner. Note that the Caramel Pecan Sauce makes about ¾ cup more than you will need for the scones; however, the sauce is delicious over ice cream, poached pears, or fresh figss. The sauce will keep covered in the refrigerator for up to one month.

3 cups presifted all-purpose flour

1 cup fine cornmeal

3 tablespoons sugar

2 tablespoons baking powder

1½ teaspoons salt

1 cup (2 sticks) unsalted butter, chilled and cut into small cubes

2–3 ripe pears, peeled and diced (about 2 cups)

4 eggs, lightly beaten

⅔ cup milk

1 egg, lightly beaten with 1 teaspoon cold water

4½ cups Caramel Pecan Sauce (see recipe on facing page)

1¼ cups crème fraîche (optional)

fresh mint leaves (optional)

1. Preheat the oven to 425° F. Lightly grease a baking sheet or line it with parchment paper.

2. In a large bowl, combine the flour, cornmeal, sugar, baking powder, and salt. Cut in the butter with a pastry blender or two knives until the consistency resembles that of coarse cornmeal.

3. Toss the pears with the flour mixture until evenly coated.

4. Stir in the eggs and milk, mixing until just combined. Be careful not to overmix.

5. Turn the dough out onto a lightly floured board and use your hands to pat it into a ¾-inch-thick round. (Using a rolling pin will toughen the dough.)

6. Use a 2½-inch round biscuit cutter to cut out the scones. Place the scones on the prepared baking sheet and brush the tops with the egg and water mixture.

7. Bake for 15–20 minutes, until golden brown.

8. Serve with a dollop of the Caramel Pecan Sauce. Top with 1 tablespoon of crème fraîche and a fresh mint leaf, if desired.

Yield: 12 servings

caramel pecan sauce

1 cup firmly packed light brown sugar

1 cup (2 sticks) unsalted butter

¾ cup honey

¼ cup granulated sugar

¼ cup heavy cream

1 pound pecans

1 teaspoon vanilla extract

½ teaspoon salt

1. Place the brown sugar, butter, honey, granulated sugar, and cream in a large saucepan over high heat. Bring to a boil, stirring constantly.

2. Boil for 5 minutes, then stir in the pecans, vanilla, and salt, thinning with a little more cream, if necessary.

Note: The caramel sauce is sufficient for a generous amount per serving.

Yield: About 4½ cups

banana-cinnamon cornmeal cake

I often incorporate puréed corn into cakes to add extra sweetness and moistness without a pronounced flavor. To use this cake as a base for individual trifles, place a slice of it in a small dessert dish and sprinkle with a little sherry, if desired. Layer with fresh or frozen and thawed sliced strawberries or canned peaches, cooked vanilla pudding, and dairy-free topping.

cooking oil spray

¾ cup (1½ sticks) butter, softened

4 eggs

1¼ cups brown sugar

2 medium-sized ripe bananas, cut into chunks

½ cup vanilla yogurt

1¼ cups canned corn kernels, drained

1 tablespoon ground cinnamon

2½ cups presifted self-rising flour

½ cup self-rising cornmeal

1. Preheat the oven to 350°F. Spray a 10-inch tube pan with cooking oil and dust with flour.

2. Place the butter in the bowl of a food processor and, adding one egg at a time, process until smooth.

3. Add the sugar, process until creamy, then add the bananas and yogurt. Process until more or less smooth.

4. Add the corn and cinnamon and process until thoroughly combined. Transfer the mixture to a large bowl.

5. In a separate bowl, combine the flour and cornmeal, then gradually fold the mixture into the butter mixture.

6. Transfer the batter to the prepared pan. Bake for about 55 minutes, or until a toothpick inserted into the cake comes out clean. Remove from the oven and cool in the pan on a wire rack for 10 minutes. Remove from the pan to a plate and cool completely before cutting.

Yield: 16–20 servings

APPENDICES

a sampling of sweet corn varieties

some of the sweetness in corn is genetically determined and is due, in part, to recessive mutants of the starchy gene found in field corn and to crossbreeding to introduce the sugary extender gene or the supersweet shrunken gene. Sweet corn is good for eating fresh and for canning and freezing. Modern varieties are classified as normal sugary (SU), supersweet or shrunken (SH2), and sugary enhanced (SE) or sugary extended (SE+).

These varieties differ in tenderness, flavor, sweetness, and the rate at which the sugar is converted to starch. With its creamy texture and sweet "corn" flavor, normal sugary corn is the standard corn grown for processing and eating fresh. Supersweets produce crisp, tender kernels with sugar concentrations two to three times higher than those of standard sweet corn varieties. Their extended shelf life makes them the most desirable types of corn for shipping long distances. Sugary enhanced corn has a creamy texture and good "corn" flavor. The kernels are very tender and sweet, because the sugar is slow to convert to starch after harvest. This corn is ideal for local and regional markets and is a favorite at roadside stands.

Although corn aficionados who grew up eating standard sweet corn, such as Golden Bantam, Silver Queen, Platinum Lady, and Butter and Sugar, bemoan the fact that modern sweets don't have that true corn flavor, many of today's corn lovers applaud the crunchy crisp texture and almost candy-sweet flavor of sugary enhanced and supersweet varieties, such as Crisp N Sweet, Kandy Korn, Even Sweeter, How Sweet It Is, and Sugar Snow.

recommended varieties: sweet corn for every palate

Yellow Kernels

Normal Sugary (SU)
Early season: Earlivee, Northern Vee, Seneca Horizon
Main season: Golden Bantam, Jubilee, Seneca Chief, Sunglow
Late season: Arrestor, Cornucopia, Jubilee

Supersweet (SH2)
Early season: Northern X-tra Sweet, X-tra Sweet 82
Main season: Super Sweet Jubilee, Sweetie 82
Late season: Illini X-tra Sweet, Paradise

Sugary Enhanced (SE)
Early season: Bodacious, Early Glow, Maple Sweet, Seneca Daybreak, Spring Treat, Sugar Buns, Tuxedo
Main season: Incredible, Kandy King, Miracle
Late season: Kandy Korn, Tendertreat

White Kernels

Normal Sugary (SU)
Main season: Platinum Lady, Stardust
Late season: Silver Queen

Supersweet (SH2)
Main season: Crystal Cream, Snowmass, Sweet Ice
Late season: How Sweet It Is, Pegasus, Snowbird, Sugar Snow

Sugary Enhanced (SE)
Early season: Divinity, Sugar Snow
Main season: Alpine, Snow Queen
Late season: Argent, Silver King

Bicolor Kernels

Normal Sugary (SU)
Early season: Quickie
Main season: Butter and Sugar
Late season: Honey 'n Frost

Supersweet (SH2)
Early season: Snowy Sun, Sweet-Green bi-70
Main season: Honey and Pearl, Monte Carlo
Late season: Hudson, Phenomenal

Sugary Enhanced (SE)
Early season: Ambrosia, Athos, D'Artagnan, Kiss 'n Tell, Seneca Dawn
Main season: Calico Belle, Delectable, Lancelot, Peaches and Cream

nutrition

native americans called corn *maize,* meaning "our life," because it sustained them from harvest to harvest; without it they would not have survived. (It received its botanical Latin name, *Zea mays,* "that which sustains the Mayas," by way of the Swedish botanist Linnaeus in 1737.)

Although per capita consumption of sweet corn (fresh, frozen, and canned) in North America is about 37 pounds per year, corn is still a staple food crop in Latin and South America. However, because corn is considered an incomplete protein, a solely corn-based diet is inadequate for total human health. To create a complete-protein meal, you must combine corn with legumes (beans or peas); nuts (including peanut butter); seeds; or small amounts of animal protein, such as milk, cheese, yogurt, eggs, meat, fish, or poultry. Mexican dishes, for example, often combine corn with rice, beans, or dairy (sour cream or cheese). Corn muffins are a complete protein because they include milk and eggs.

Besides tasting delicious, corn provides high-quality nutrition. As a complex carbohydrate, it is an energy booster. Even vegetable haters love corn's sweet, nutty, and creamy flavors. And, when harvested, stored, and cooked properly, corn is also juicy, crisp, and tender. The bonus, of course, is that corn also contains most vitamins and minerals, at least in small amounts. It is a source of phosphorus, iron, calcium, and riboflavin, and the cellulose hulls provide fiber. Although all corn contains traces of vitamin A (natural beta-carotene) and vitamin C, yellow corn contains higher concentrations of both vitamins than white corn does.

The countdown: One kernel is approximately 71 percent carbohydrates, 10 to 14 percent water, 10.5 percent protein, 3 percent fat, and 1.5 percent fiber. One medium ear of fresh sweet corn equals ½ cup of kernels and contains 70 calories. One large ear of yellow corn is approximately 77 grams, equals ⅔ cup of kernels, and provides 11 percent of the recommended daily allowance of thiamine, 3 grams of protein, and 85 calories. One large ear of white corn is approximately 90 grams and provides 80 calories, 1 gram of fat, 10 milligrams of sodium, 19 grams of carbohydrates, 1 gram of dietary fiber, 8 grams of sugar, 3 grams of protein, and 4 percent vitamins. Food scientists have found that boiling corn in water can destroy half of the vitamin C content. However, microwaving preserves most of the vitamin C. The caloric content of super-sweet corn is pretty much the same as that of standard sweet corn and does not decline as kernels age and lose their sweetness.

resources

the growing latin american population in the United States has contributed to the wide range of corn products now available at specialty stores and many supermarkets across the country. I consider myself lucky — I live in northern Virginia, where there is a growing community of Latin Americans. I can walk into any supermarket and find *masa harina* (traditional corn flour), canned hominy (rehydrated, dried corn kernels), and yellow, white, and blue cornmeal. I also live in a region where old gristmills are enjoying public and government support. The renovated Aldie Mill in Loudoun County, Virginia, provides me with a regular source of freshly ground white and yellow cornmeal. If don't live in a region enriched by Hispanic or Latin American culture and cuisine, you can order many corn products — blue cornmeal, *masa harina*, pancake and biscuit mixes, whole dried kernels, canned *posole*, corn husks, corn tortillas, tortilla presses, and more — through catalogs and Web sites.

Arrowhead Mills

P.O. Box 2059
Hereford, TX 79045
Tel: (800) 749-0730
www.arrowheadmills.com
Stone-ground corn

Bob's Red Mill Natural Foods

5209 SE International Way
Milwaukie, OR 97222
Tel: (800) 349-2173
Fax: (503) 653-1339
www.bobsredmill.com
Stone-ground corn

Butte Creek Mill

P.O. Box 561
402 Royal Avenue N.
Eagle Point, OR 97524
Tel: (541) 826-3531
Fax: (541) 830-8444
www.buttecreekmill.com
Cornmeal, stone-ground mixes, and gift boxes

Café Atlántico

405 8th Street NW
Washington, DC 20004
Tel: (202) 393-0812
Fax: (202) 393-0555
http://207.115.30.124/index.htm
Recipes featured on pages 63, 95, and 146

Casa Lucas

2934 24th Street
San Francisco, CA 94110
Tel: (415) 826-4334
Fax: (415) 826-7985
Ingredients and equipment for making tortillas

Colvin Run Mill

10017 Colvin Run Road
Great Falls, VA 22066
Tel: (703) 759-2771
Fax: (703) 759-7490
www.colvinrunmill.org
Stone-ground corn

John Cope's Food Products

156 W. Harrisburg Avenue
Rheems, PA 17570
Tel: (800) 745-8211
www.copefoods.com
Dried sweet corn

Corn Maze in the Plains

4557 Old Tavern Road
The Plains, VA 20198
Tel: (540) 456-7339
www.circleofseeds.com
Organic corn maze cosponsored by Seeds of Change

FoxFire Grille

Rimfire Lodge
Snowshoe, WV 26209
Tel: (304) 572-5555
www.theredfox.com
Recipe featured on pages 80–81

Great Country Farms

18780 Foggy Bottom Road
Bluemont, VA 20135
Tel and Fax: (540) 554-2073
www.greatcountryfarms.com
Community-supported organic farm specializing in sweet and popping corns; profile and recipe featured on pages 160–61

International Tamale Festival (December)

Indio, CA
Tel: (760) 342-6532
Fax: (760) 342-6556
www.tamalefestival.org

Jerry Kinsman

Pueblo Santa Ana
2 Dove Road
Albuquerque, NM 87004
Tel: (505) 867-3301
Blue corn

Kenyon Cornmeal Co.
Usquepaugh
West Kingston, RI 02892
Tel: (800) 753-6966
Fax: (401) 782-3564
www.kenyonsgristmill.com
Cornmeal and old-fashioned mixes

Kitchen/Market
218 Eighth Avenue
New York, NY 10011
Tel: (888) 468-4433
www.kitchenmarket.com

McCrady's Restaurant
2 Unity Alley
Charleston, SC 29401
Tel: (843) 577-0025
Recipe featured on pages 136–137

Moore Fine Food
148 Main Street
Great Barrington, MA 01230
Tel: (413) 528-4500
Fax: (413) 528-6779
moore.finefood@verizon.net
Recipe featured on pages 174–175

National Corn Growers Association
1000 Executive Pkwy, Ste. 105
St. Louis, MO 63141
Tel: (314) 275-9915
Fax: (314) 275-7061
www.ncga.com
Information on corn production in the U.S.; links to state organizations

The Popcorn Factory
13970 West Laurel Drive
Lake Forest, IL 60045
Tel: (800) 541-2676
Fax: (847) 362-6464
www.thepopcornfactory.com
Popcorn gift products

Popcorn Institute
401 North Michigan Avenue
Chicago, IL 60611
Tel: (312) 644-6610
Fax: (312) 527-6658
www.popcorn.org
Popcorn information, nutrition, games, and recipes

The Red Fox Restaurant
P.O. Box 39
1 Whistlepunk Village
Snowshoe, WV 26209
Tel: (304) 572-1111
Fax: (304) 572-2222
www.theredfox.com
Recipes featured on pages 83 and 92–93

Santa Fe School of Cooking
116 West San Francisco Street
Santa Fe, NM 87501
Tel: (800) 982-4688
www.santafeschoolofcooking.com
Cooking school and ethnic food market specializing in Southwestern cuisine; recipe featured on pages 152–53

War Eagle Mill
11045 War Eagle Road
Rogers, AR 72756
Tel: (479) 789-5343
Fax: (479) 789-2972
www.wareaglemill.com
Cornmeal, stone-ground mixes, and gift boxes

Williams-Sonoma, Inc.
3250 Van Ness Avenue
San Francisco, CA 94109
Tel: (800) 541-2233
Fax: (702) 363-2541
www.williams-sonoma.com
Cooking equipment and supplies and food products

World Grits Festival (April)
St. George, SC
Tel: (843) 563-4366
www.turnersouth.com/grits

index

Other Storey Titles You Will Enjoy

101 Perfect Chocolate Chip Cookies, by Gwen Steege. The chocolate chip cookie is North America's favorite cookie, and with 101 unique recipes to choose from, readers are sure to find their own favorite version, or two, or three! Also includes tips for making perfect chocolate chip cookies every time. 144 pages. Paperback. ISBN 1-58017-312-8.

Apple Cookbook, by Olwen Woodier. More than 140 recipes put everyone's favorite fruit into tasty new combinations. Also includes easy instructions for canning and freezing apples and applesauce. 144 pages. Paperback. ISBN 1-58017-389-6.

The Big Book of Preserving the Harvest, by Carol W. Costenbader. New techniques for canning, freezing, juicing, pickling, drying, and storing fresh foods so you can enjoy their delicate flavors all year long. 352 pages. Paperback. ISBN 1-58017-458-2.

The Classic Zucchini Cookbook, by Nancy C. Ralston, Marynor Jordan, and Andrea Chesman. Includes more than 190 delicious and healthful recipes focusing on zucchini, summer squash, edible gourds, and other squash. 304 pages. Paperback. ISBN 1-58017-453-1.

Maple Syrup Cookbook, by Ken Haedrich. This cookbook offers a repertoire of more than 100 recipes featuring maple syrup as the sweetening ingredient. Includes recipes for breakfast, starters, entrées, baked goods, desserts, beverages, butters, relishes, and more. 144 pages. Paperback. ISBN 1-58017-404-3.

Pickles and Relishes, by Andrea Chesman. Readers can turn their crops into mouthwatering pickles and relishes as tasty as grandma made. 160 pages. Paperback. ISBN 0-88266-744-0.

Picnic, by DeeDee Stovel. This unique cookbook offers 29 picnic event ideas with more than 125 recipes. These packable repasts for every season include traditional fare as well as soups, entrées, salads, and desserts that are a cut above the ordinary. 192 pages. Paperback. ISBN 1-58017-377-2.

These books and other Storey books are available at your bookstore, farm store, garden center, or directly from Storey Books, 210 MASS MoCA Way, North Adams, MA 01247 or by calling 1-800-441-5700. Or visit our Web site at www.storey.com